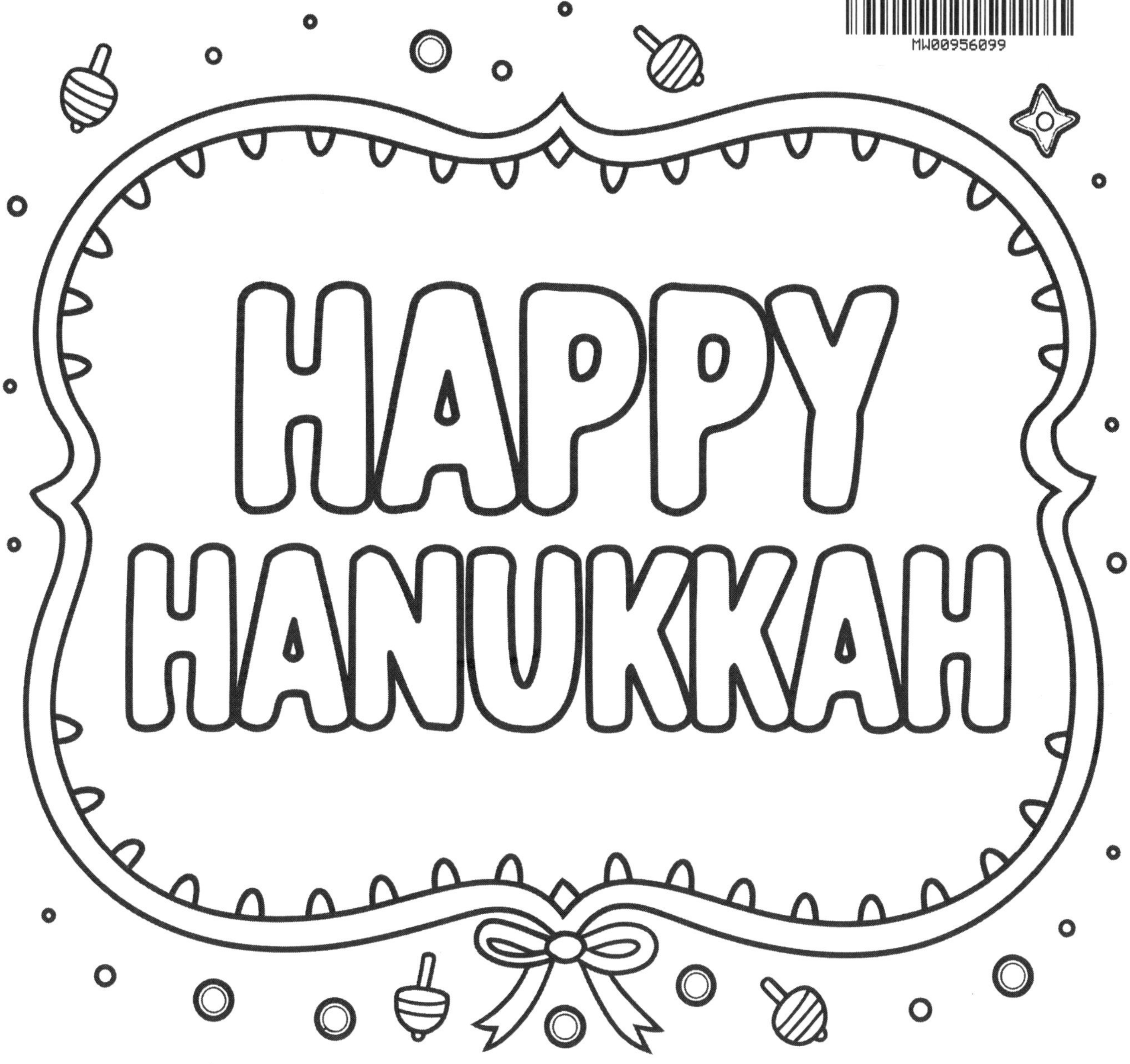
HAPPY
HANUKKAH

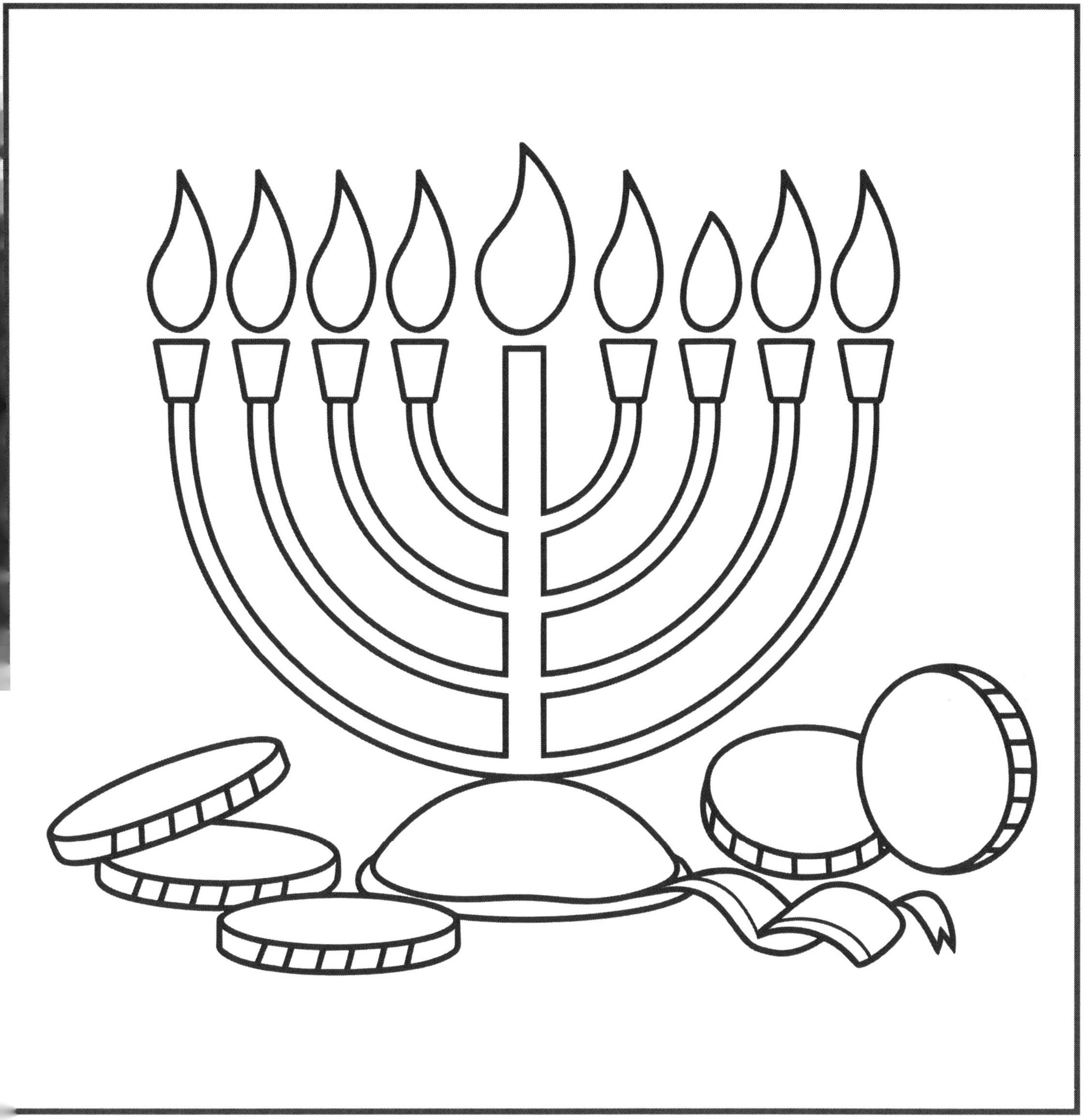

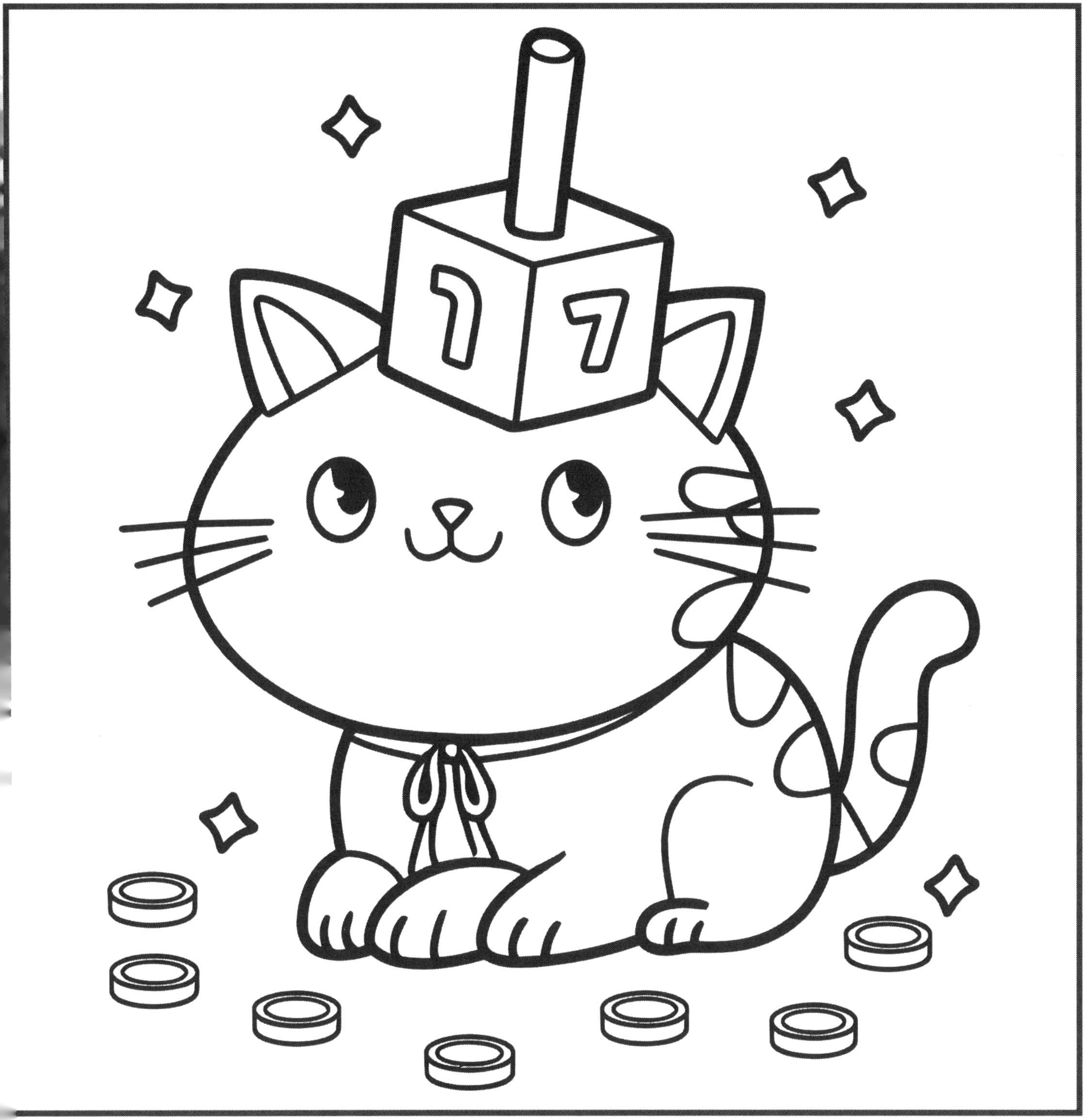

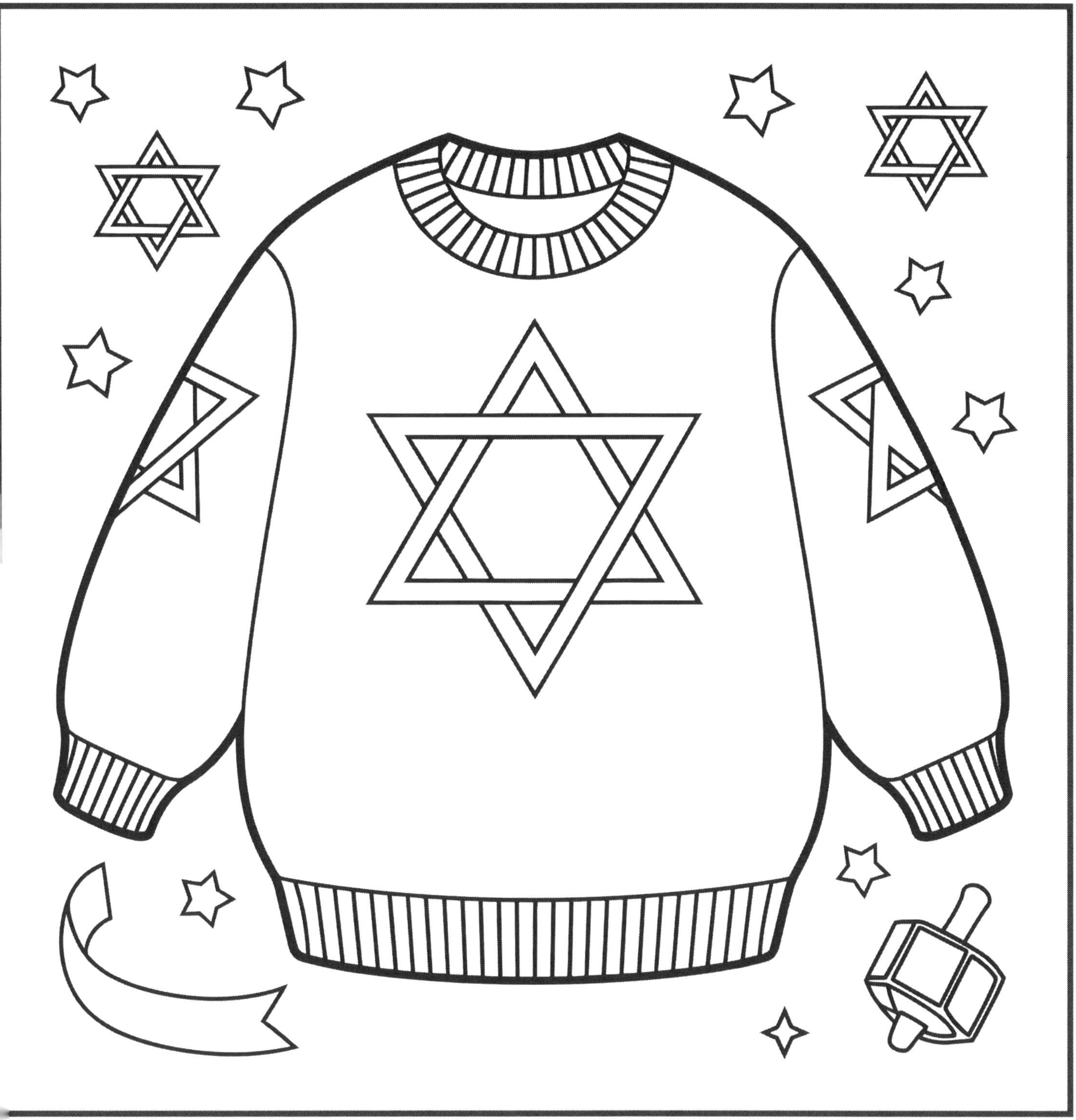

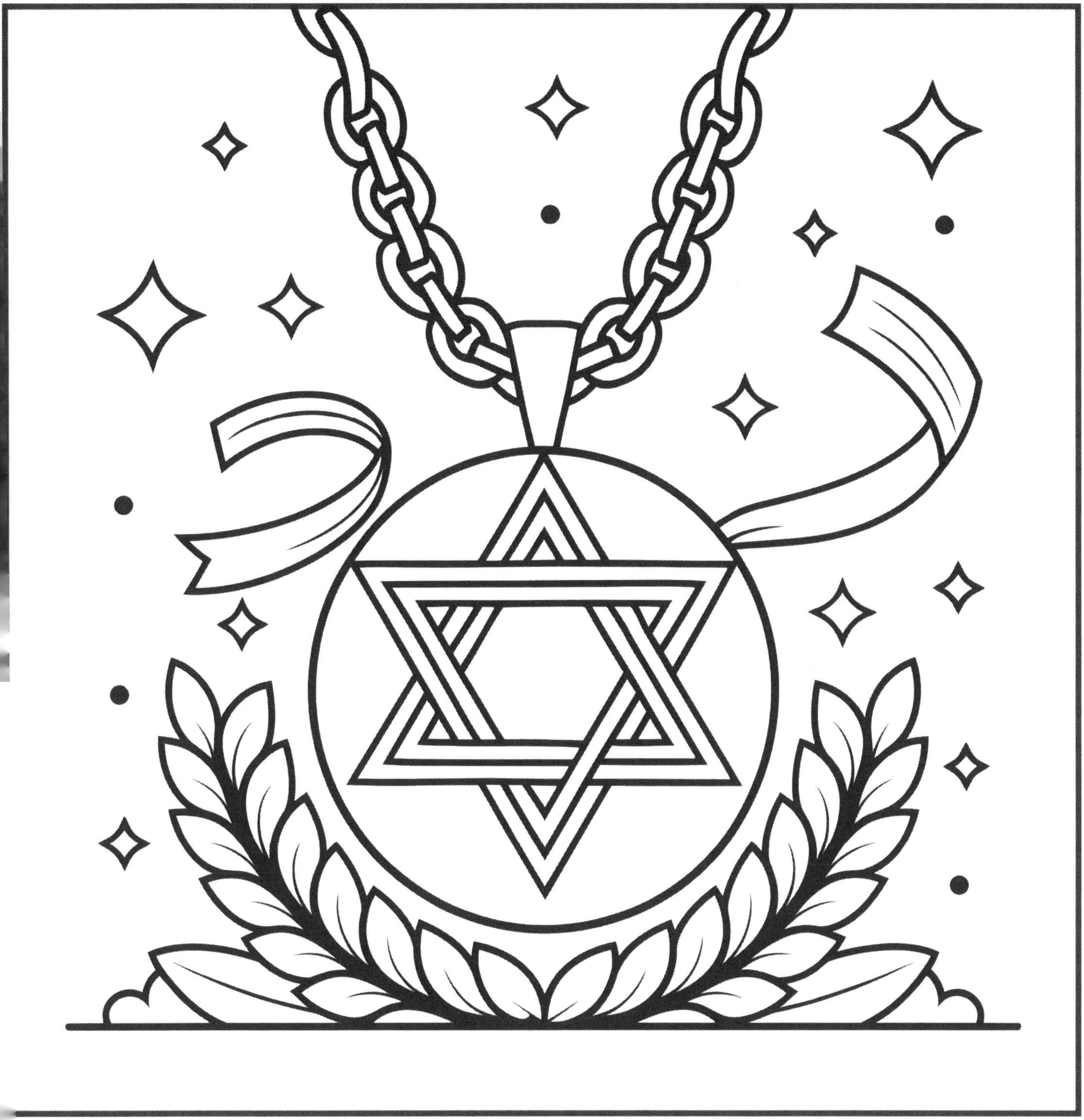

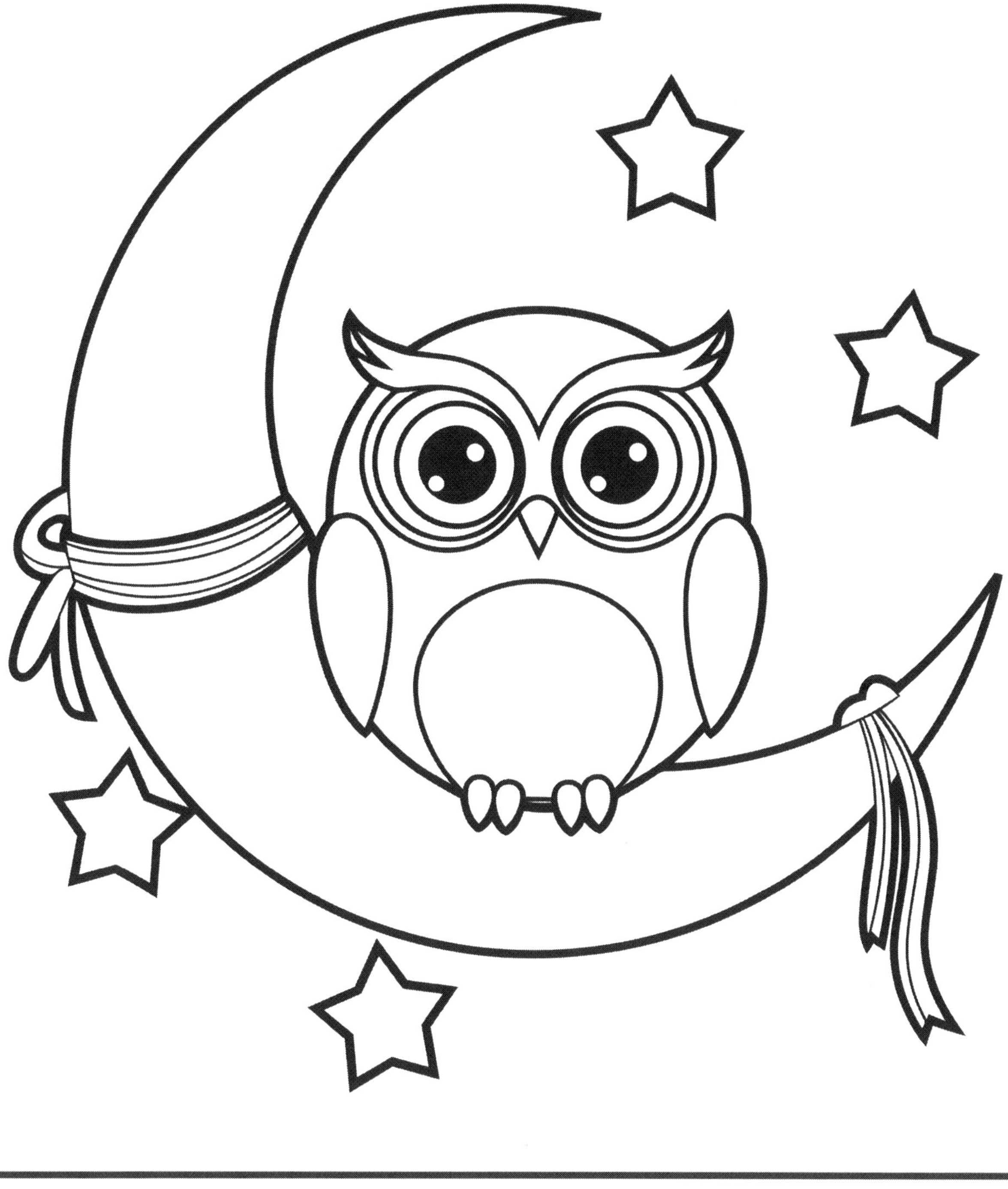

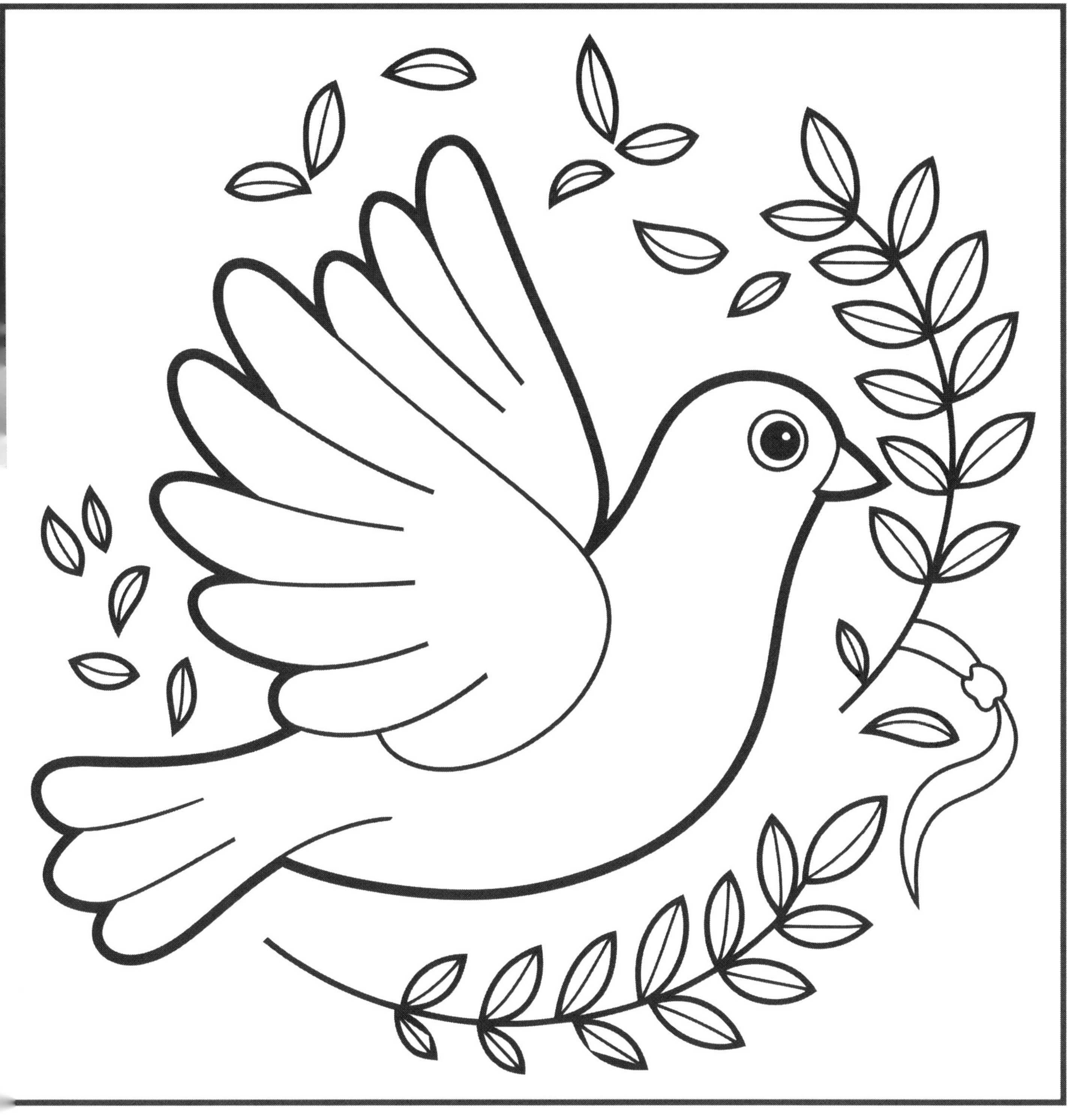

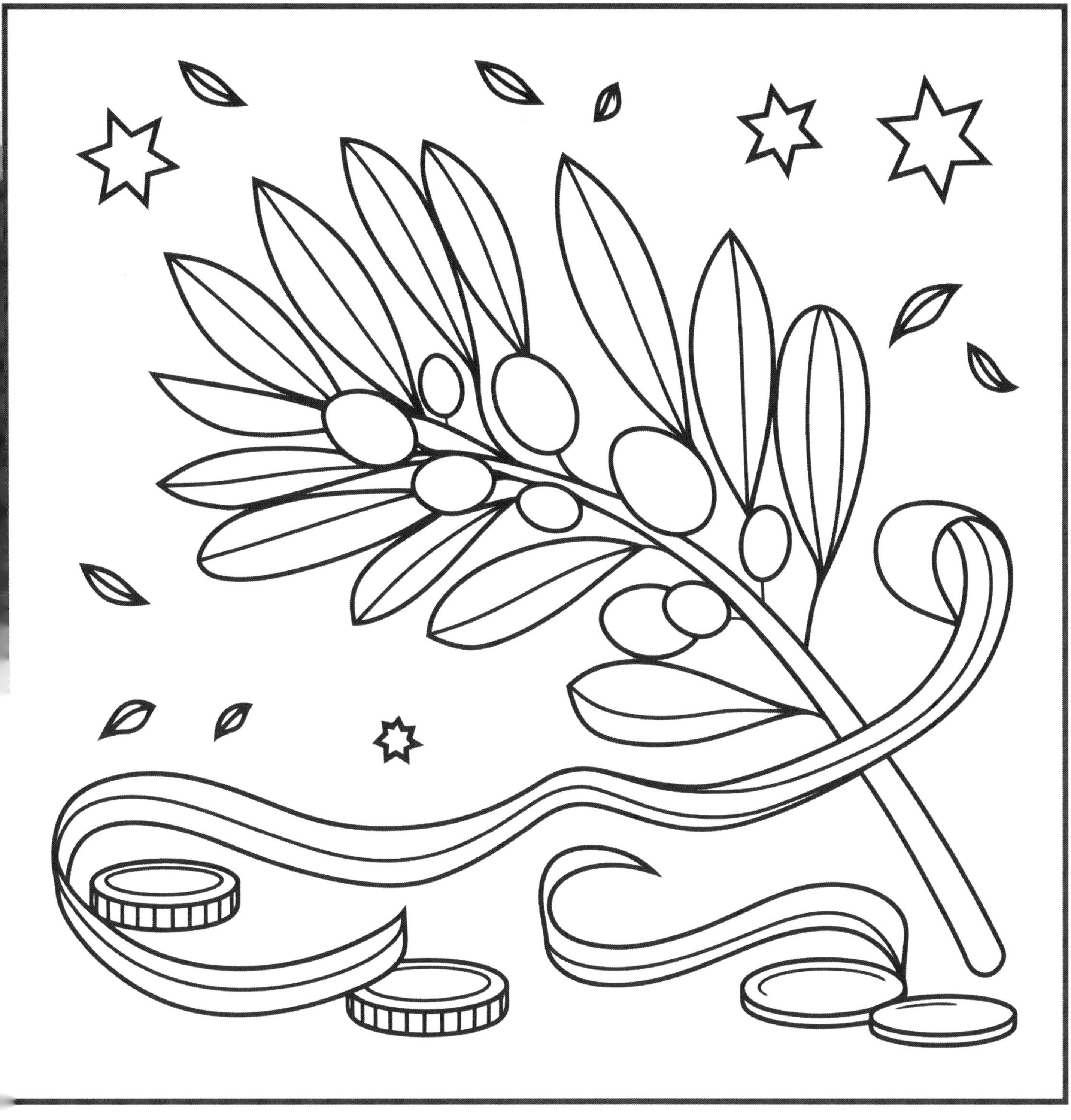

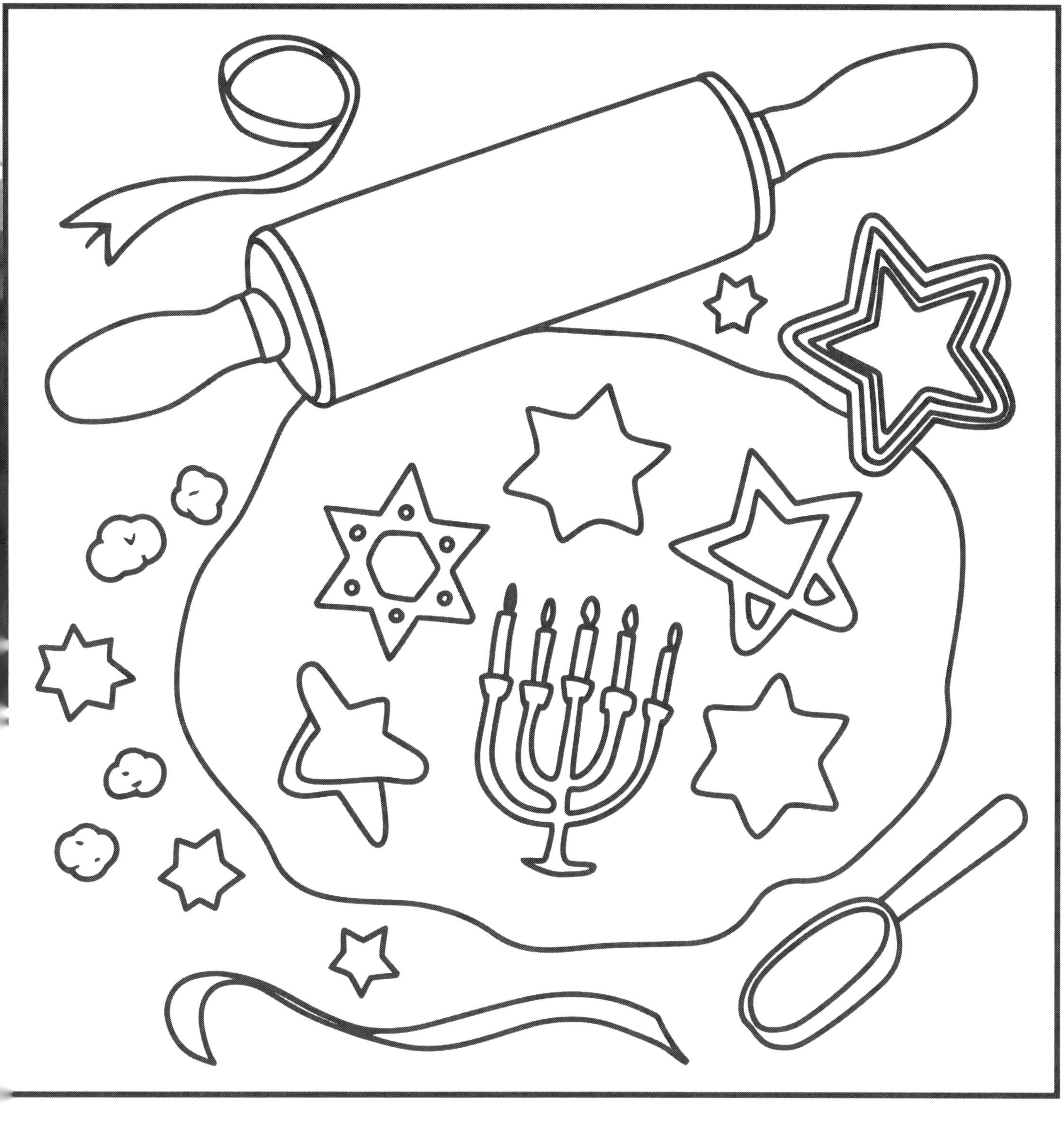

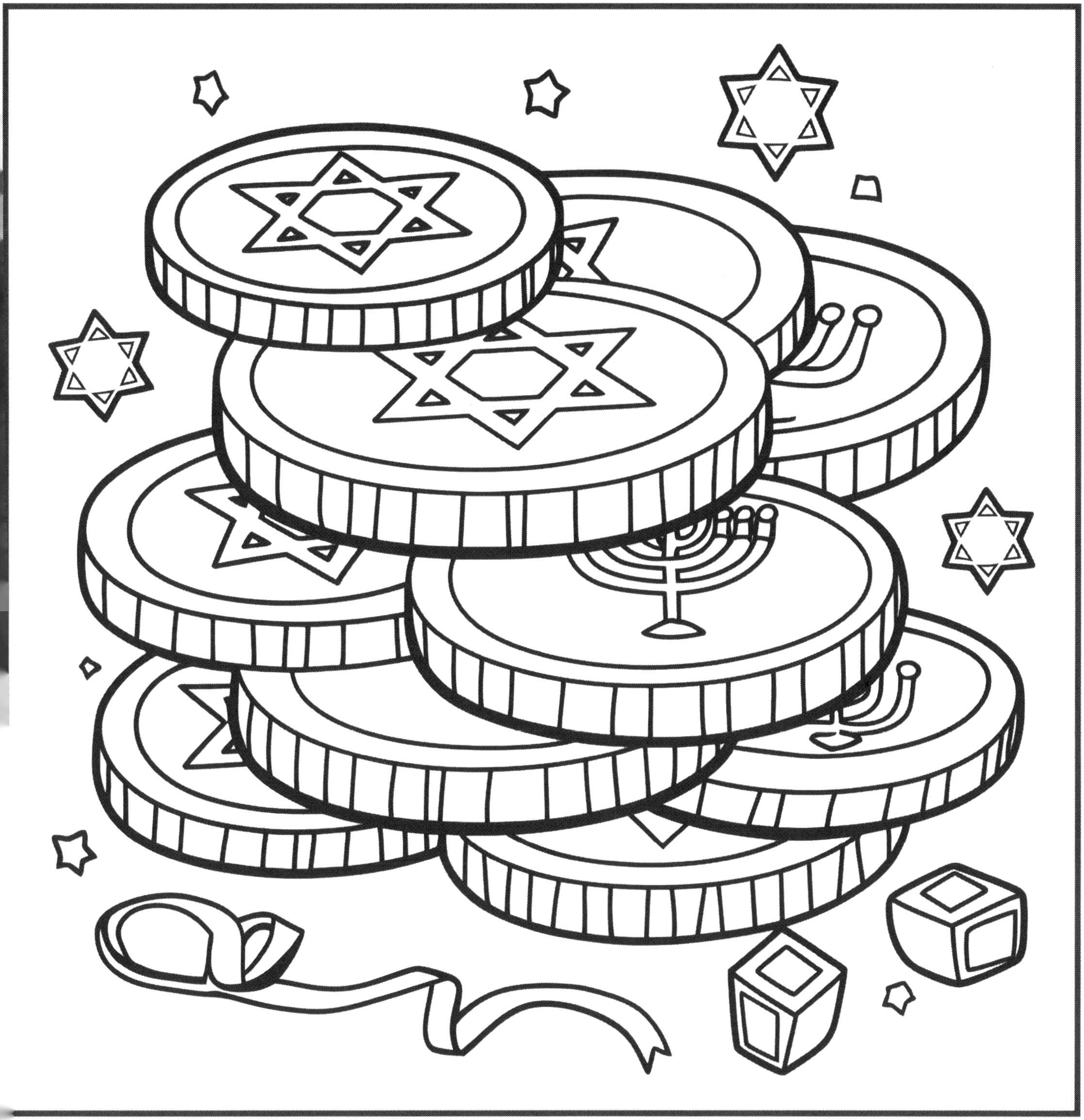

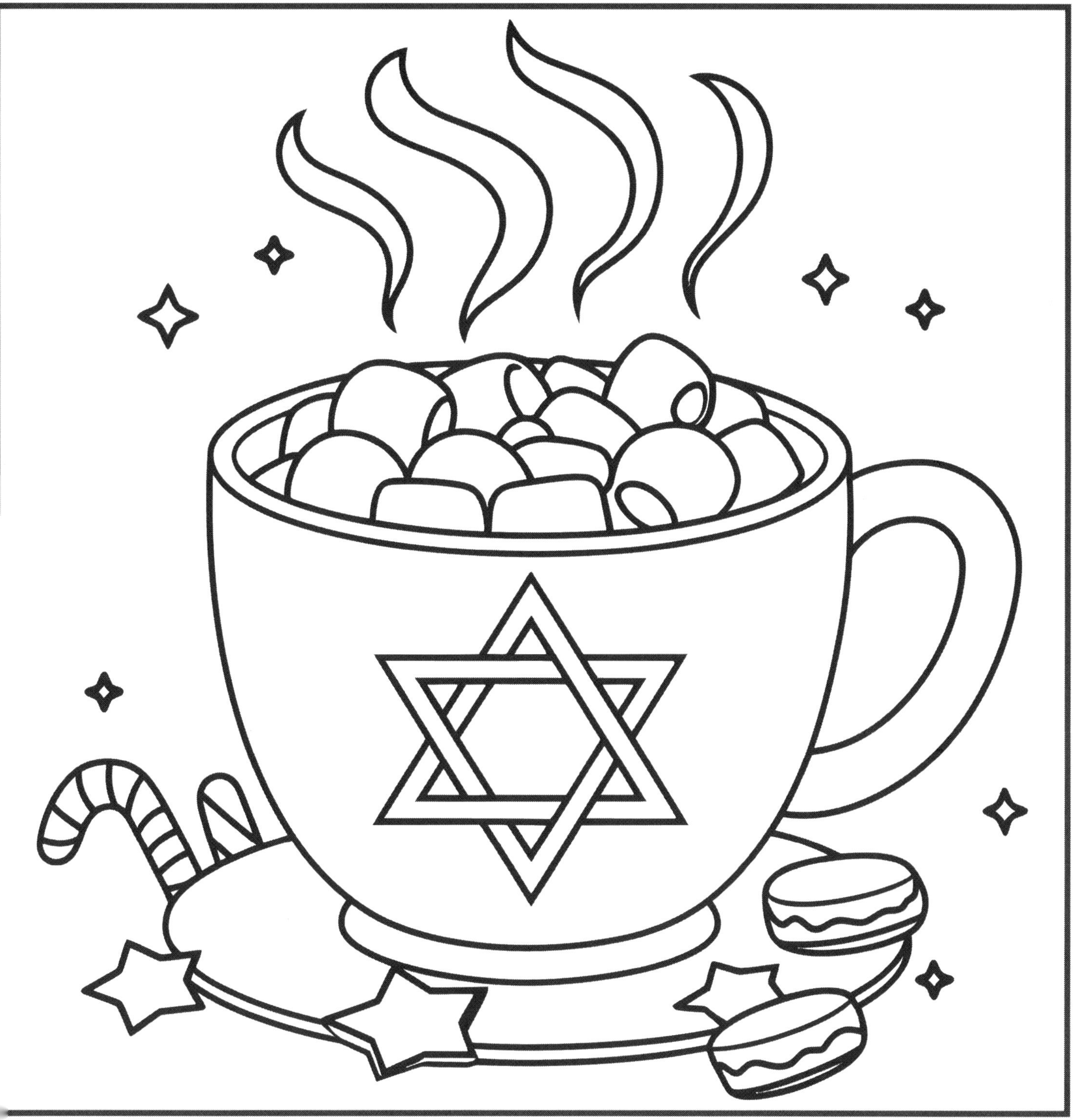

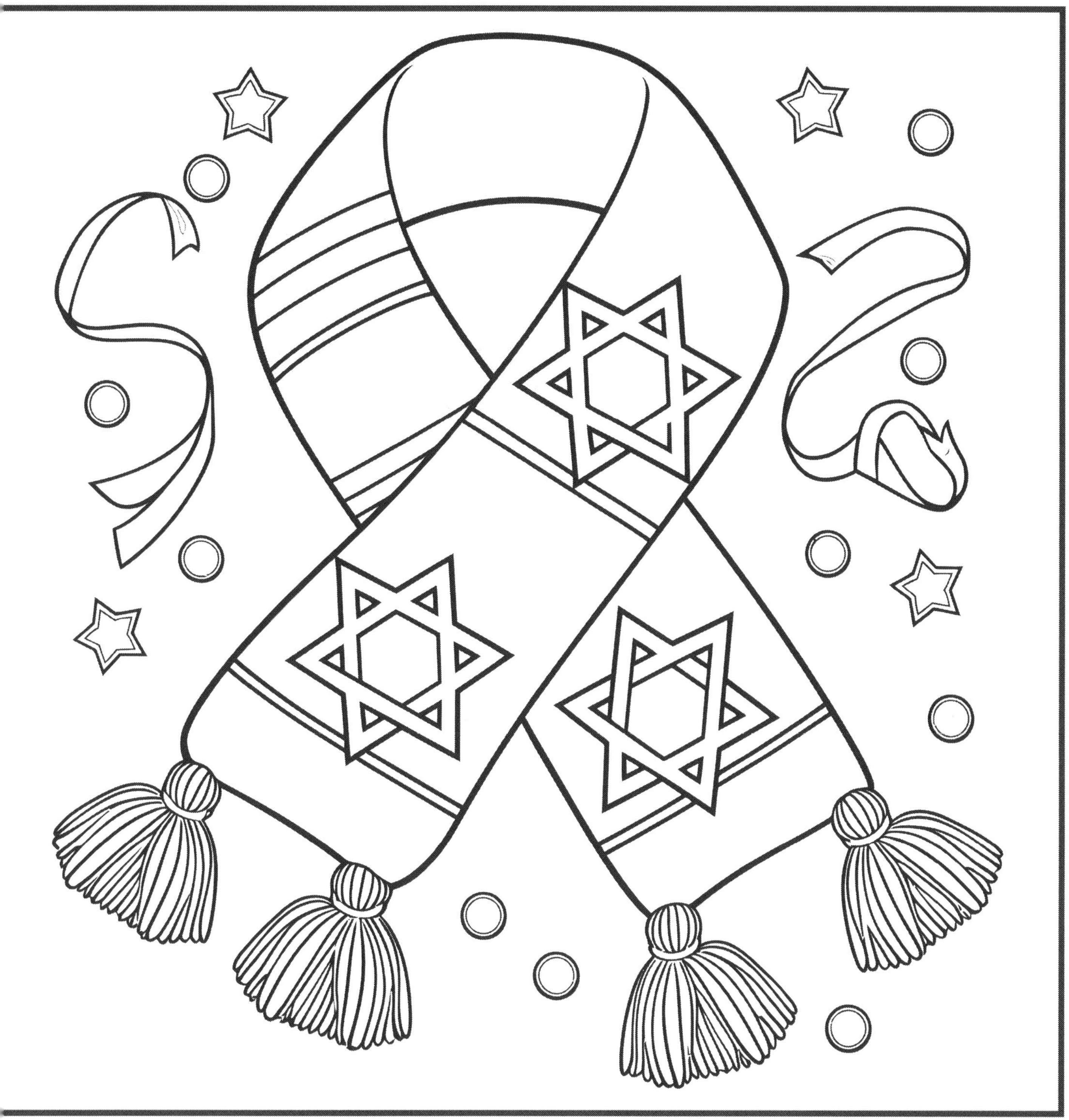

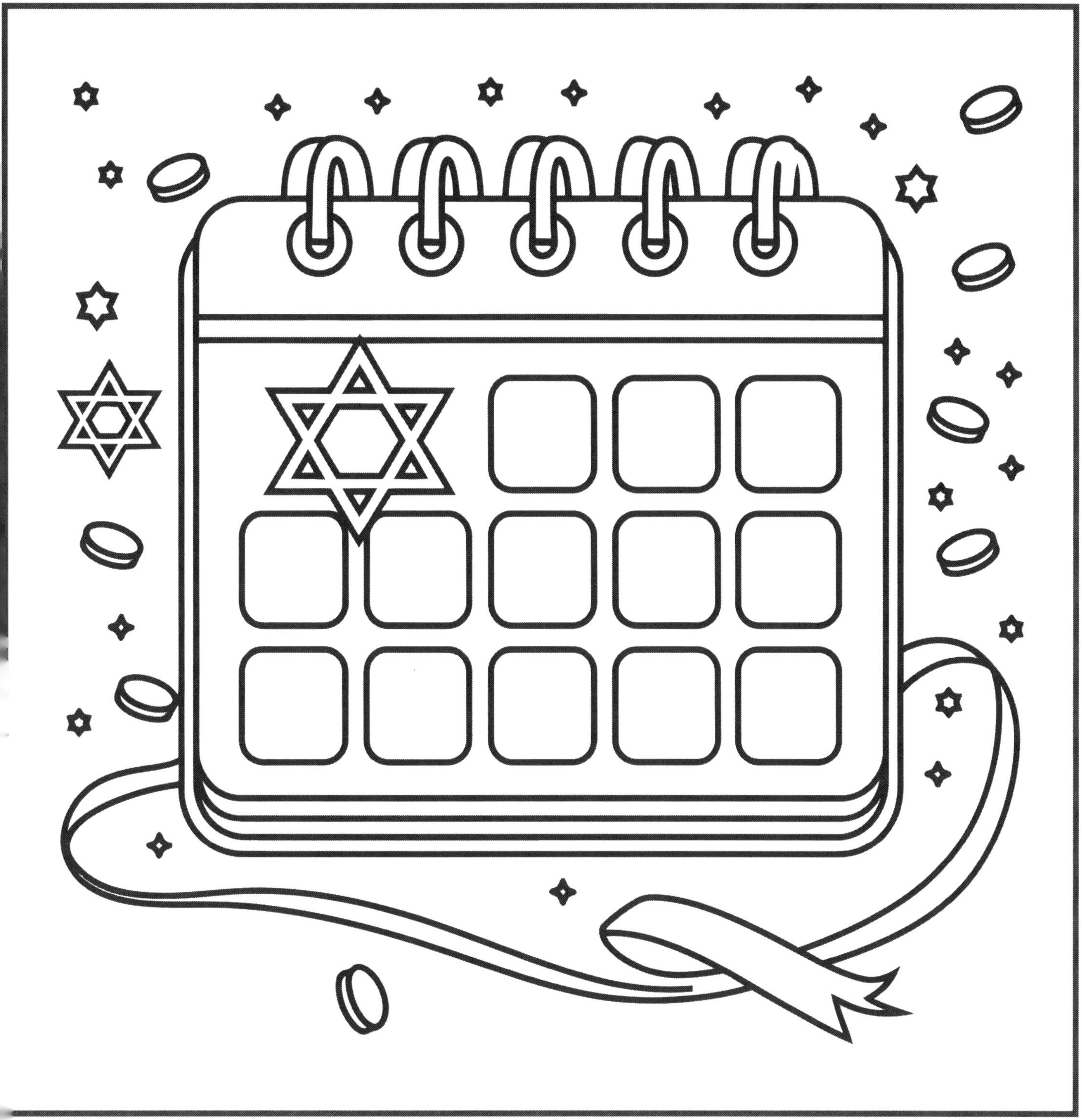

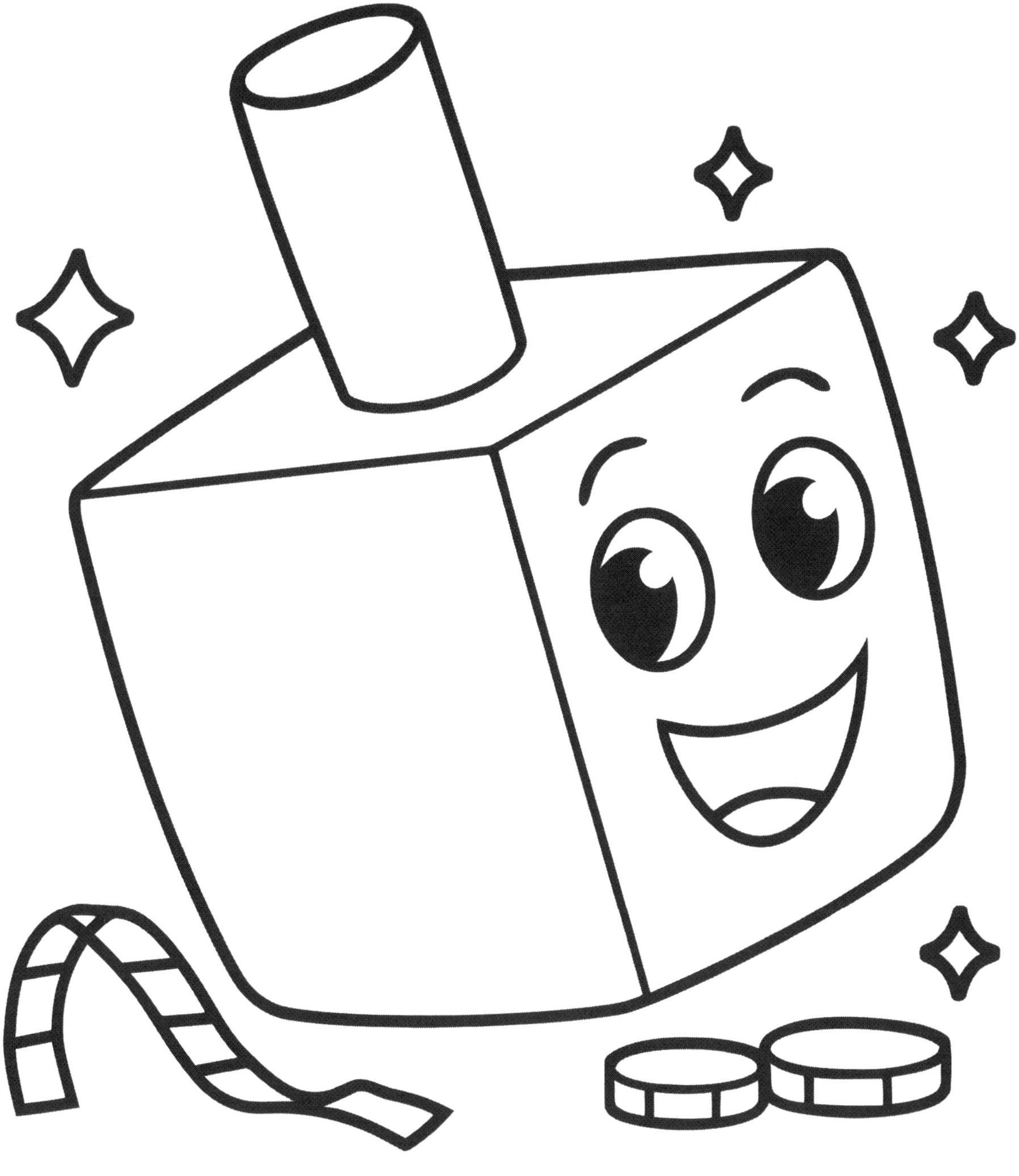

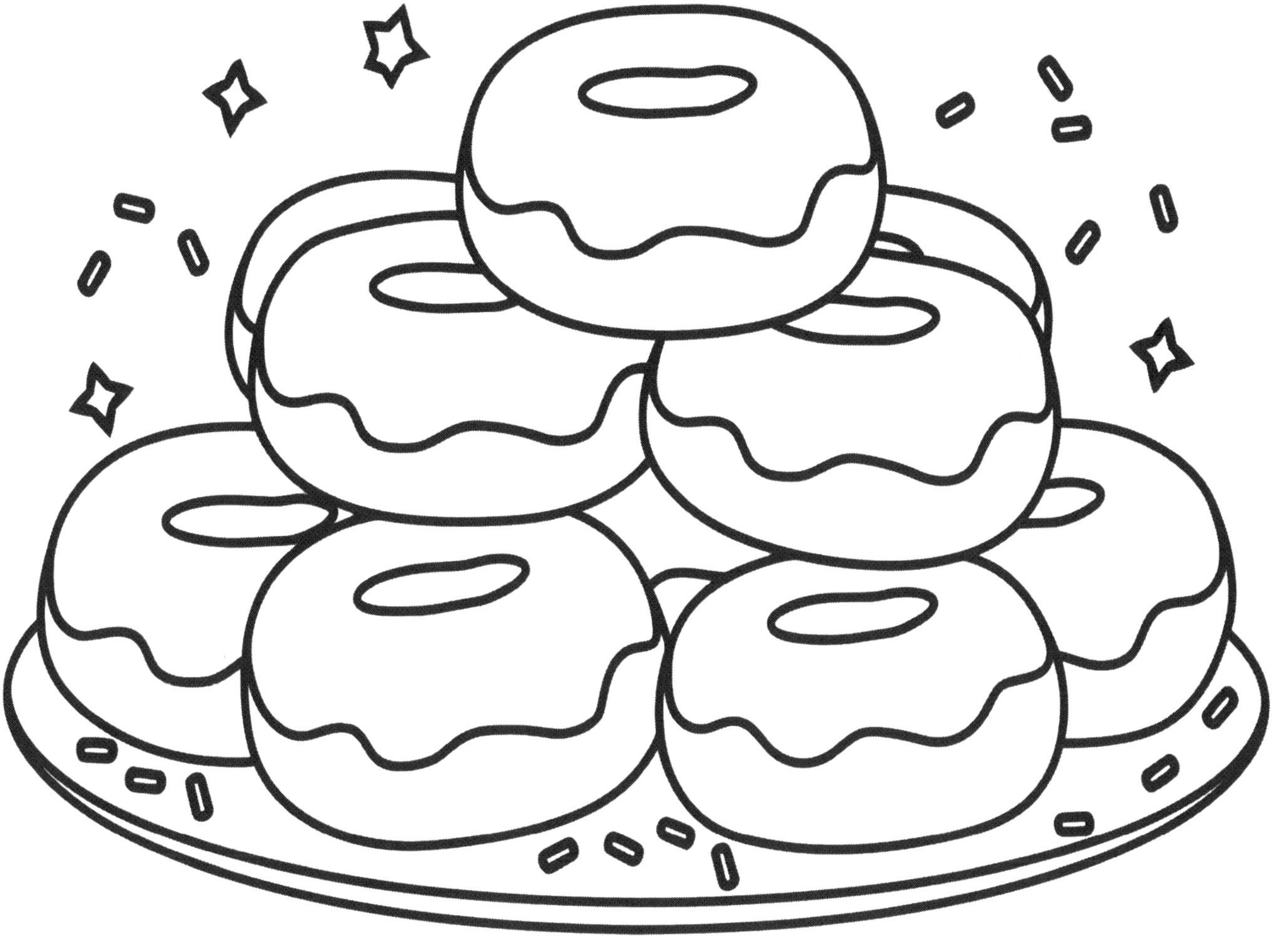

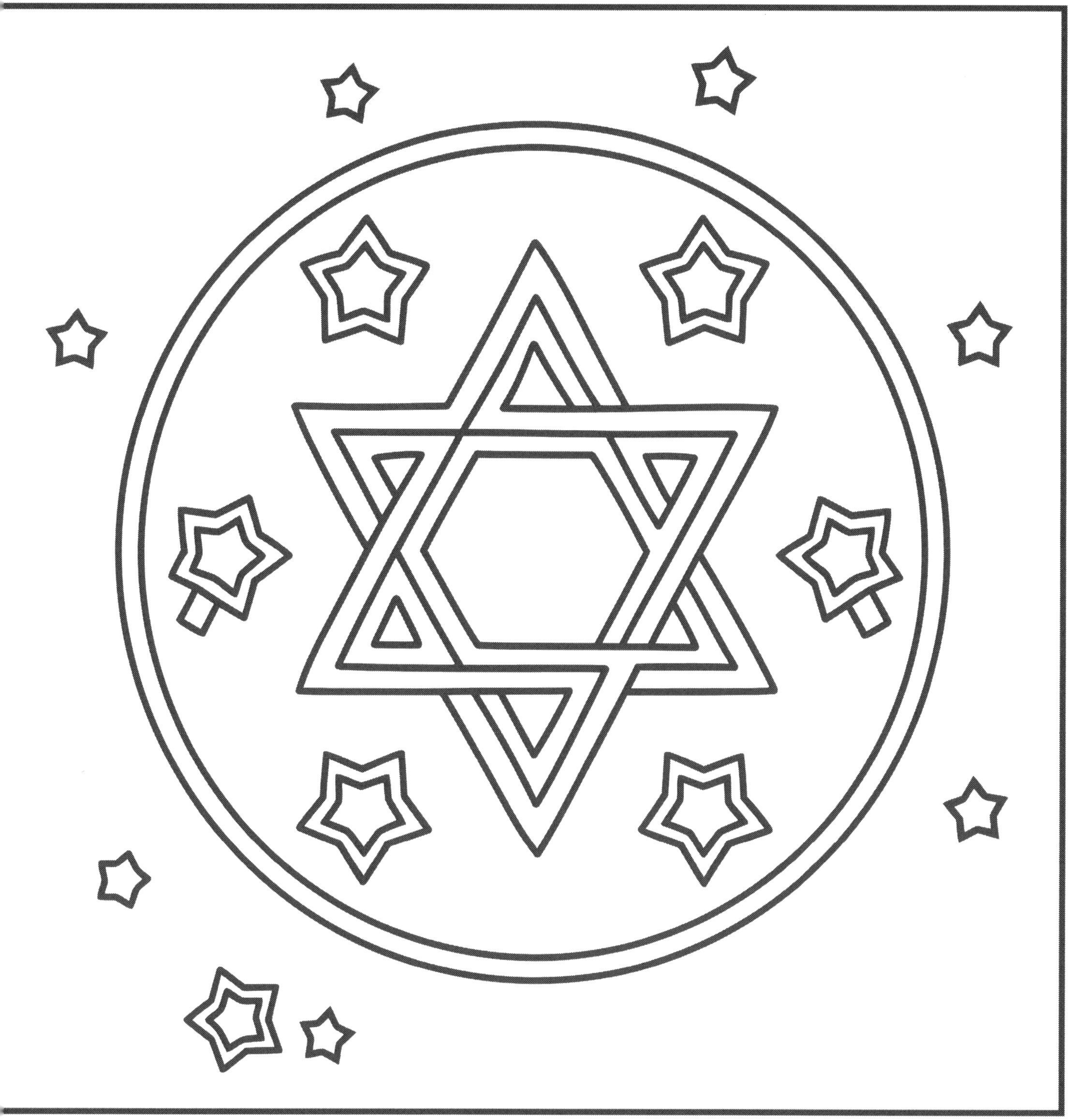

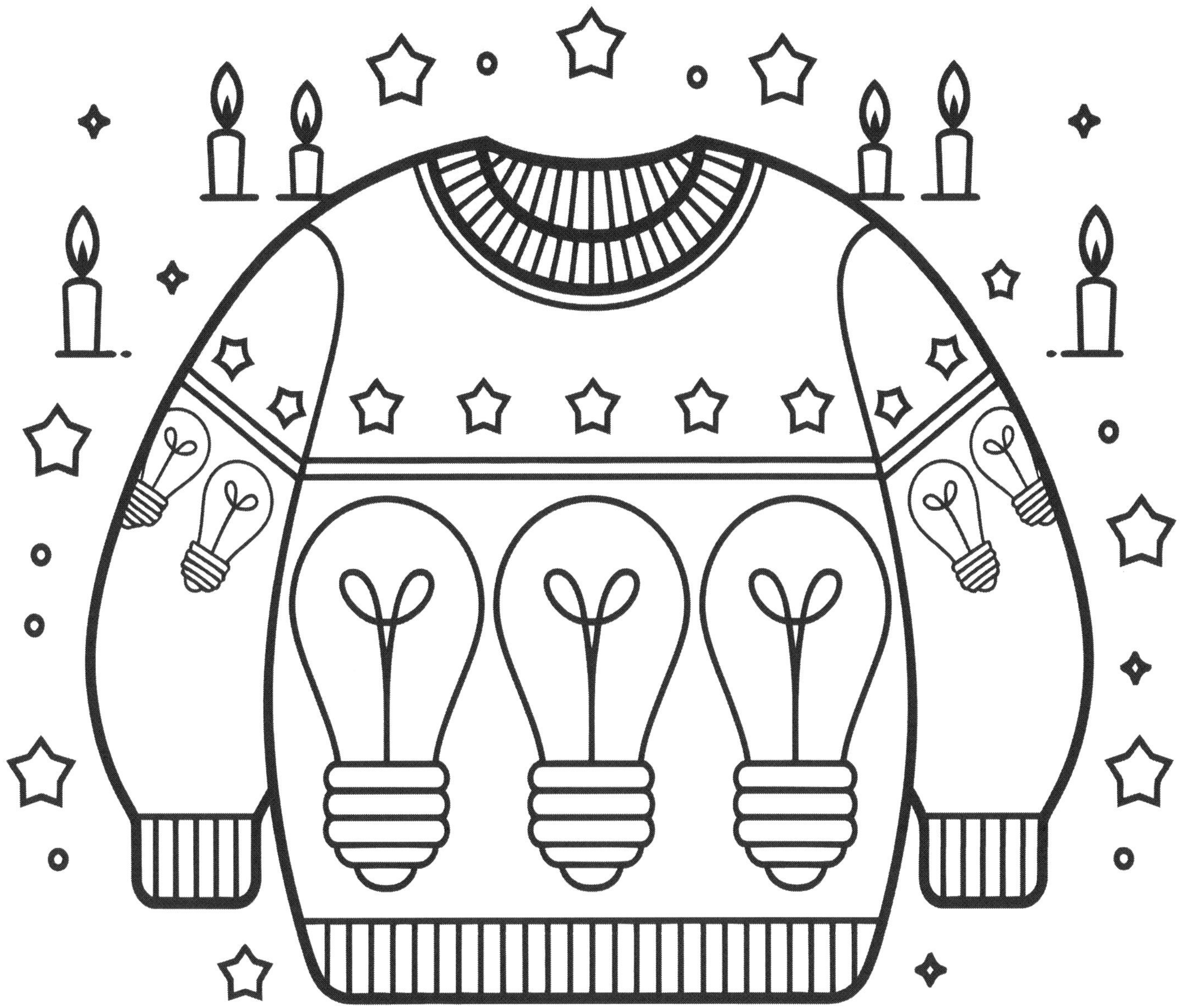

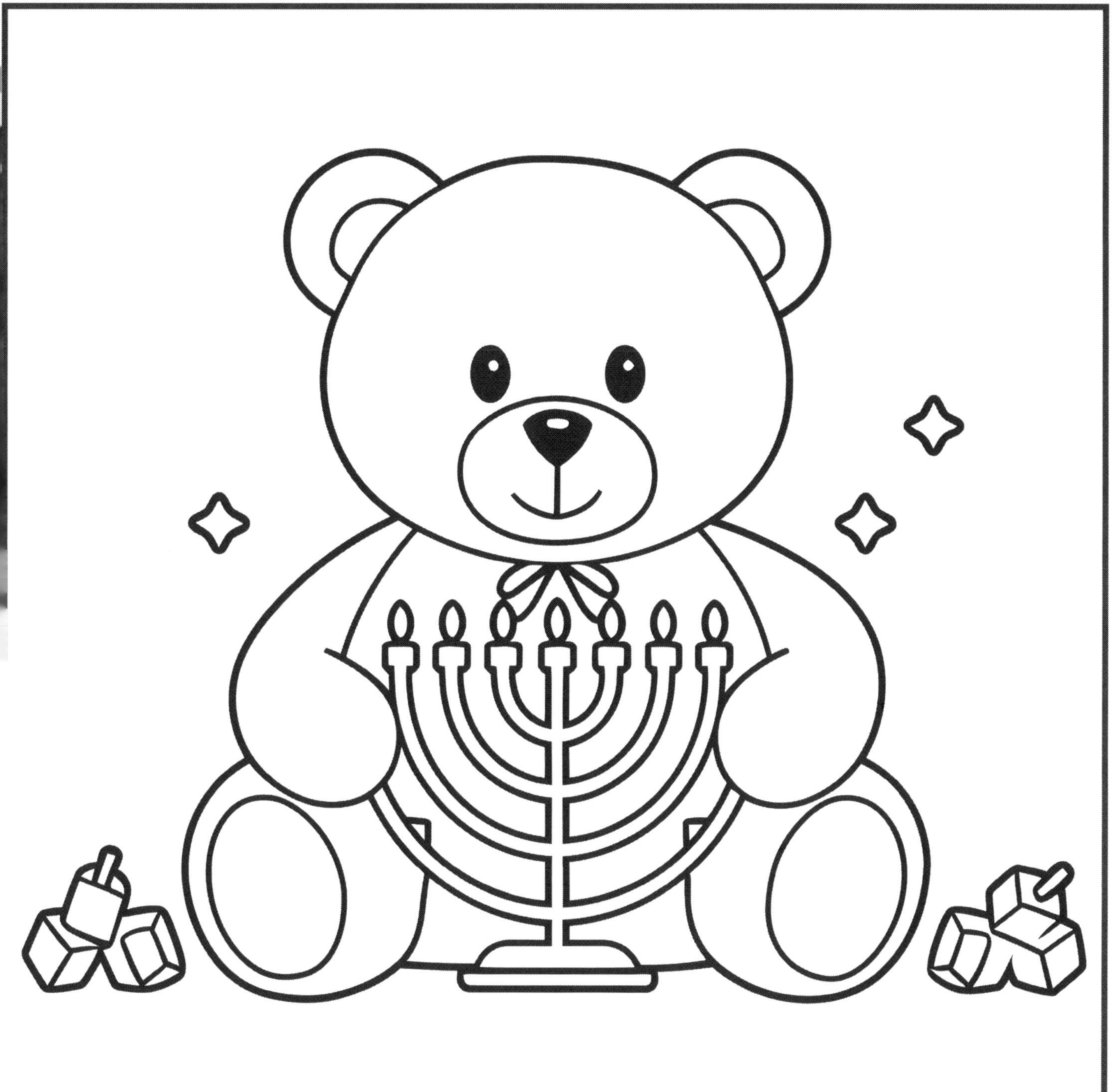

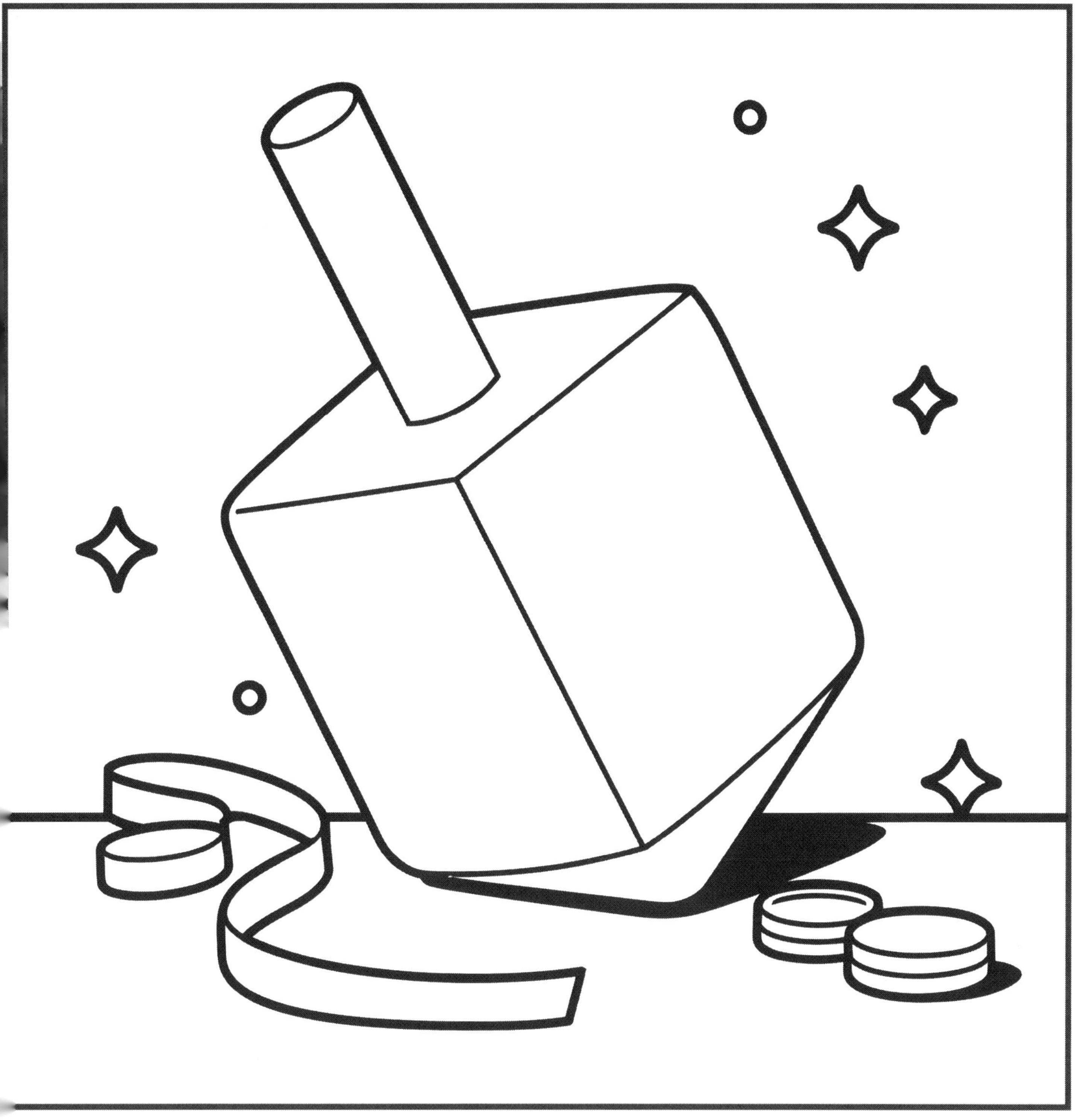

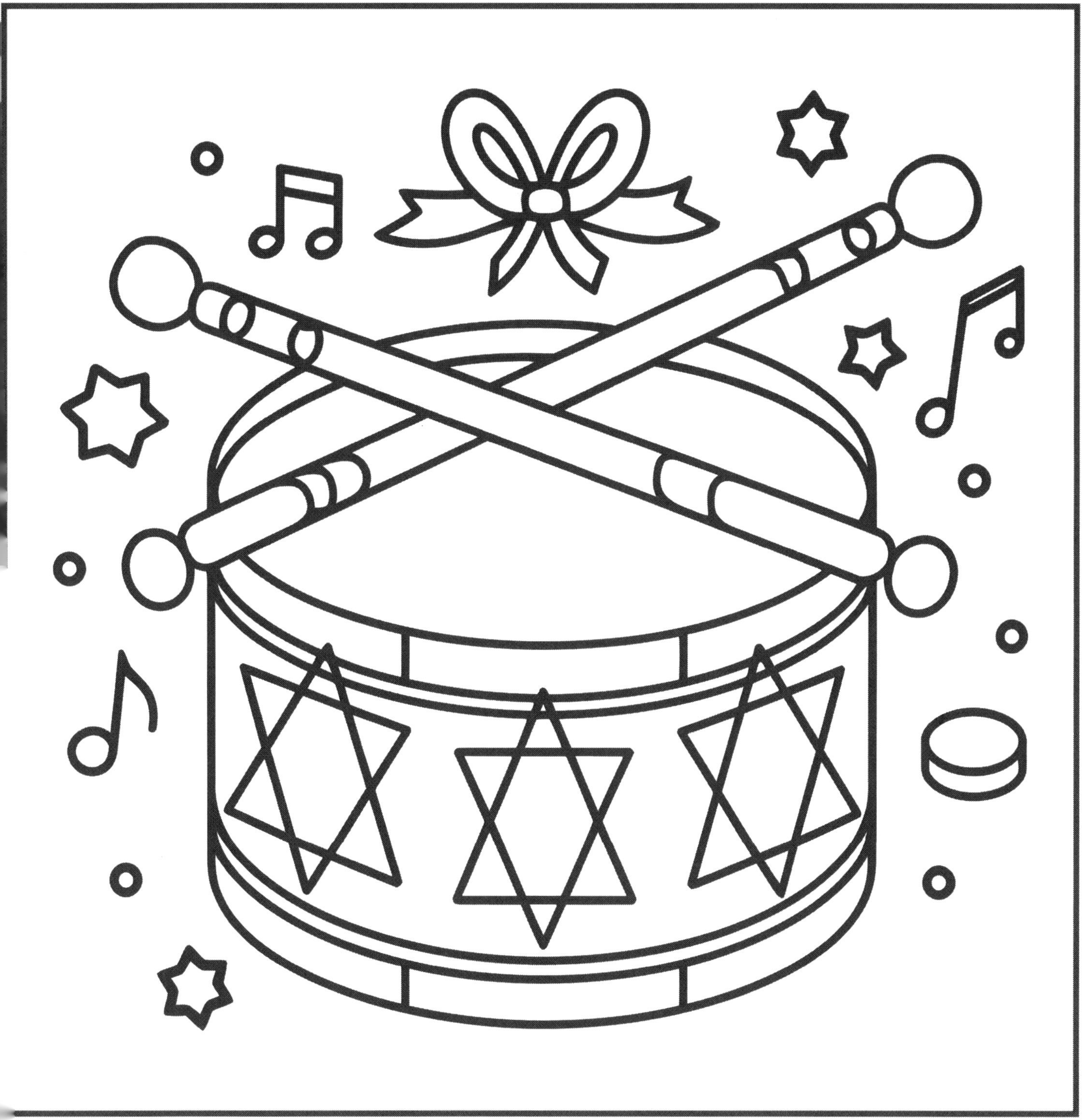

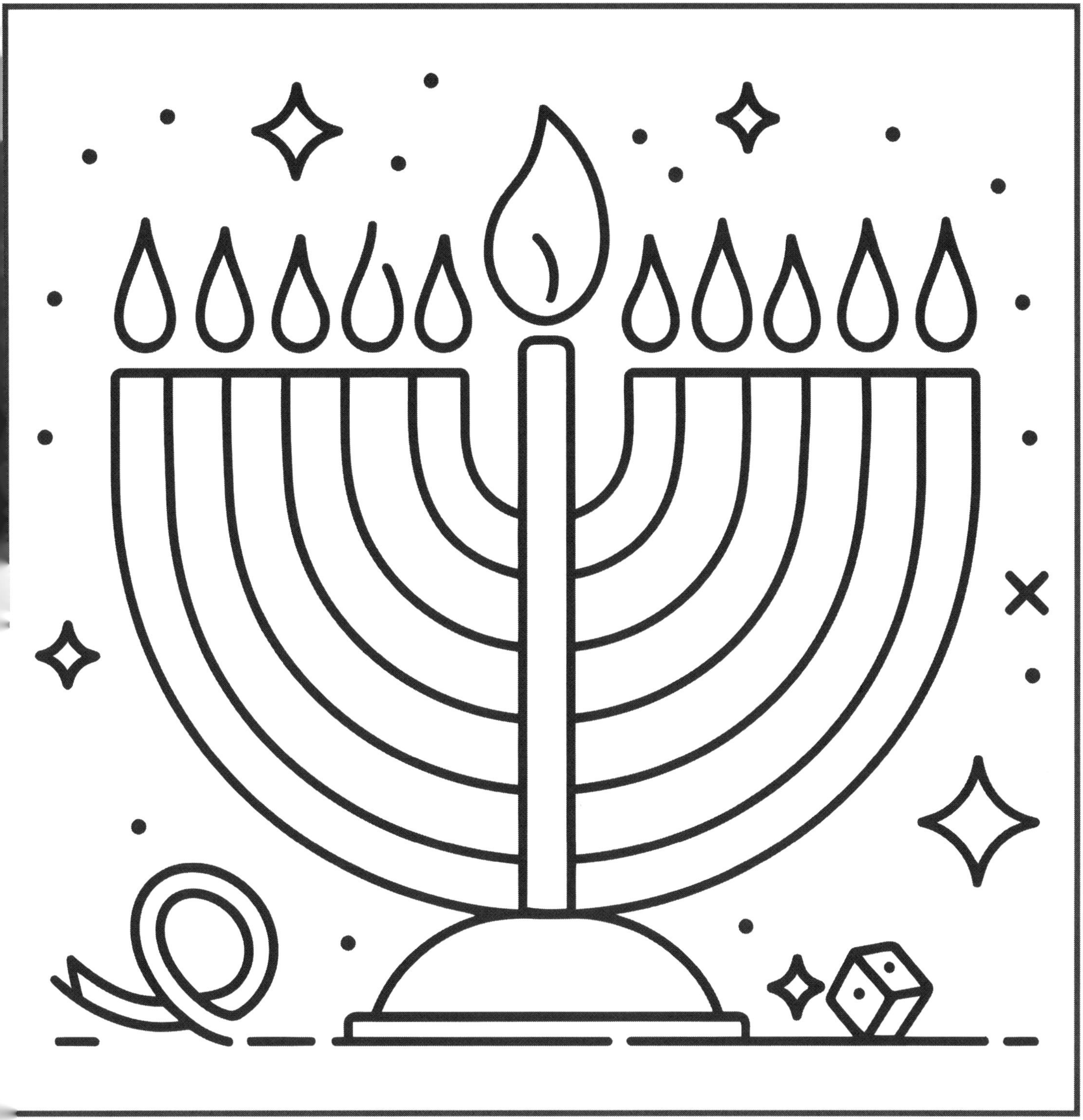

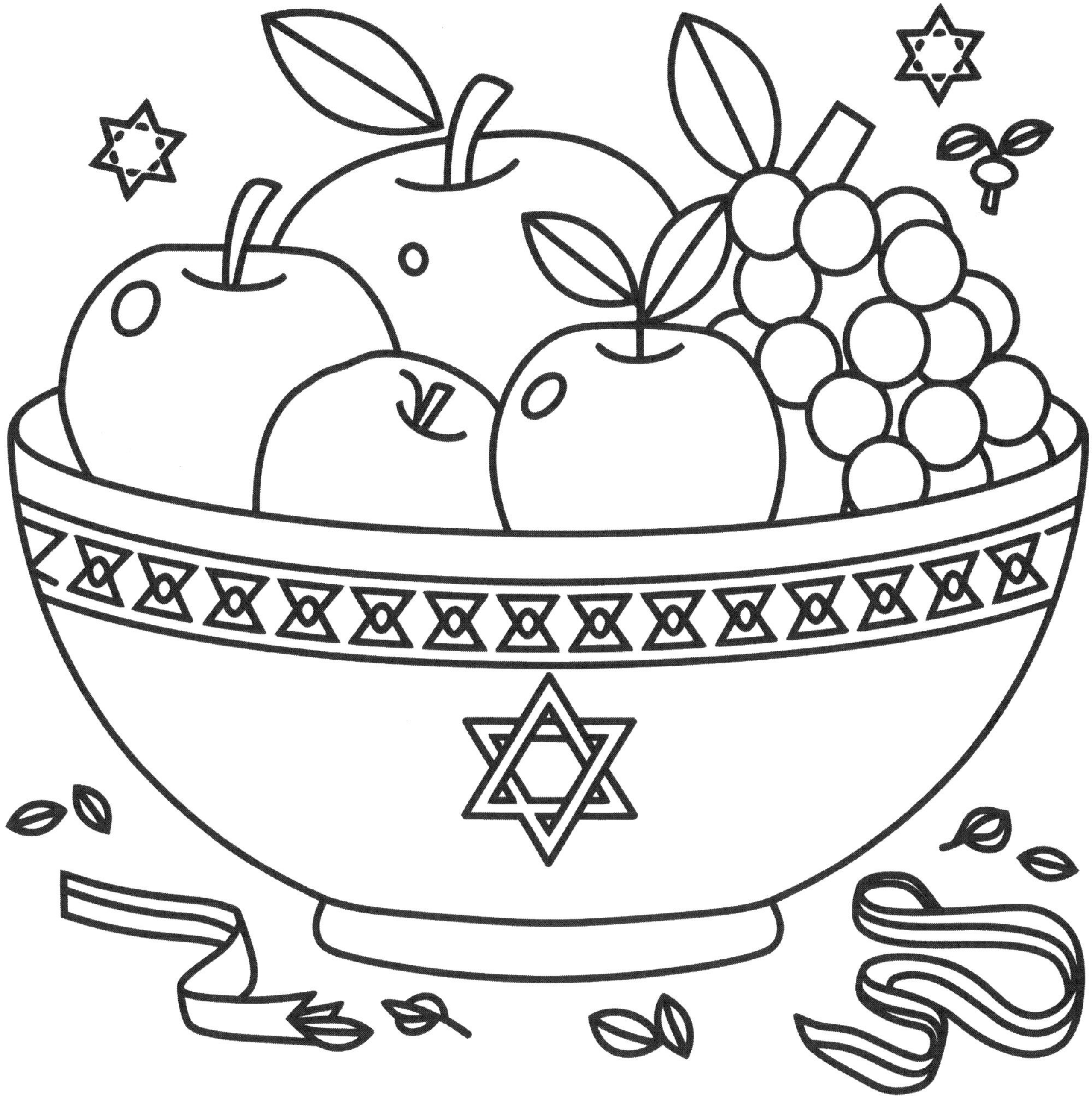

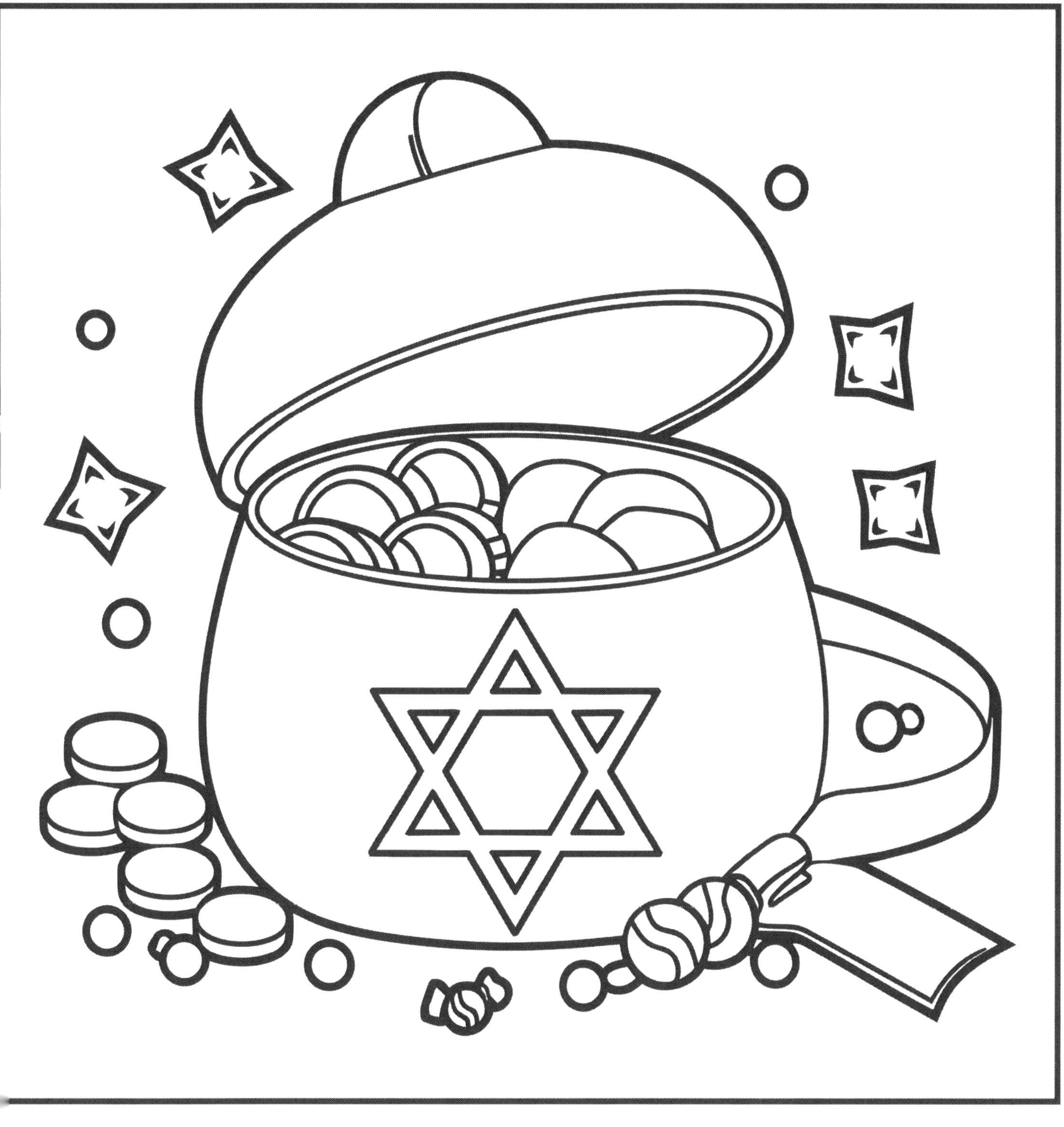

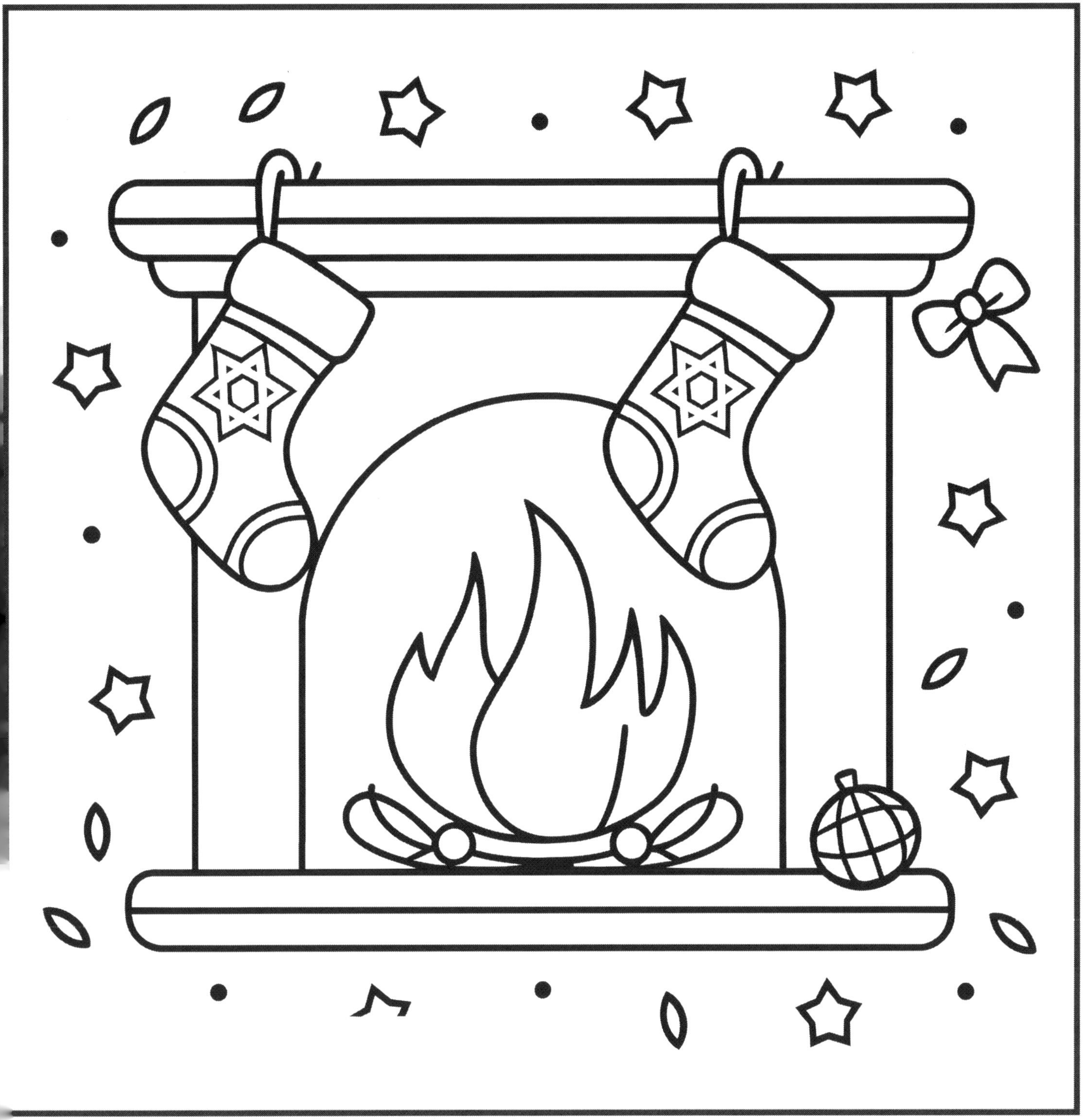

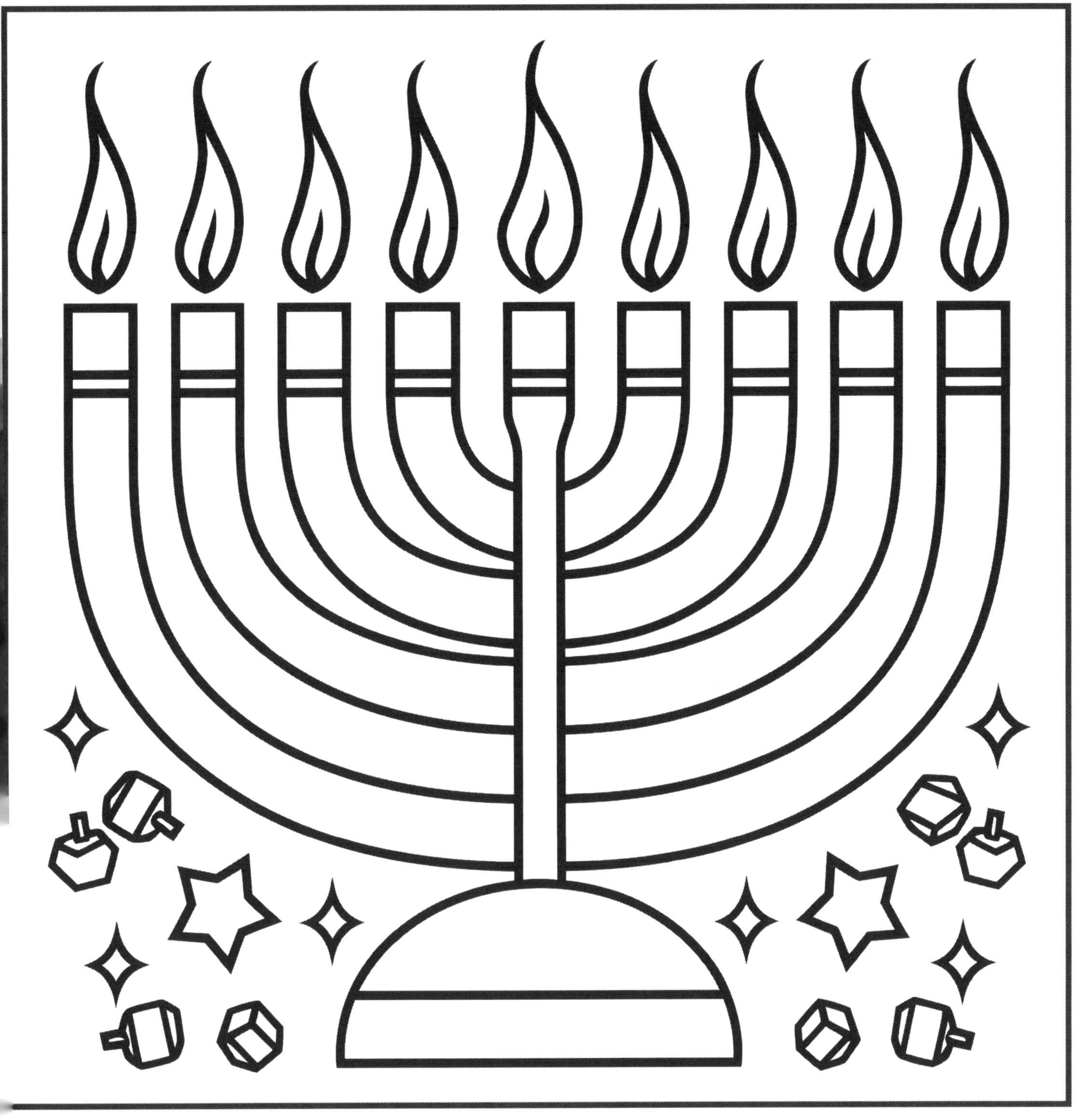

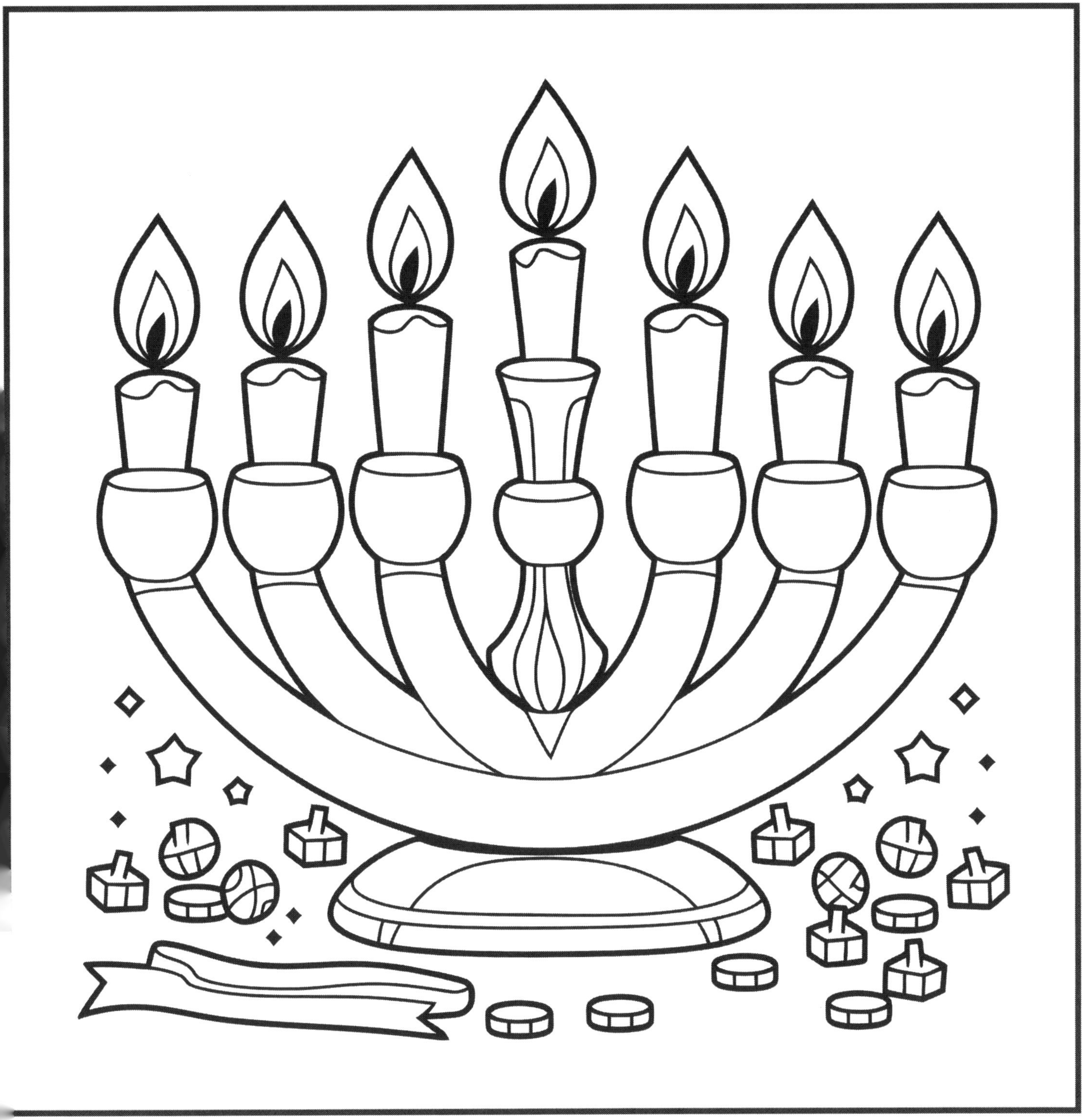

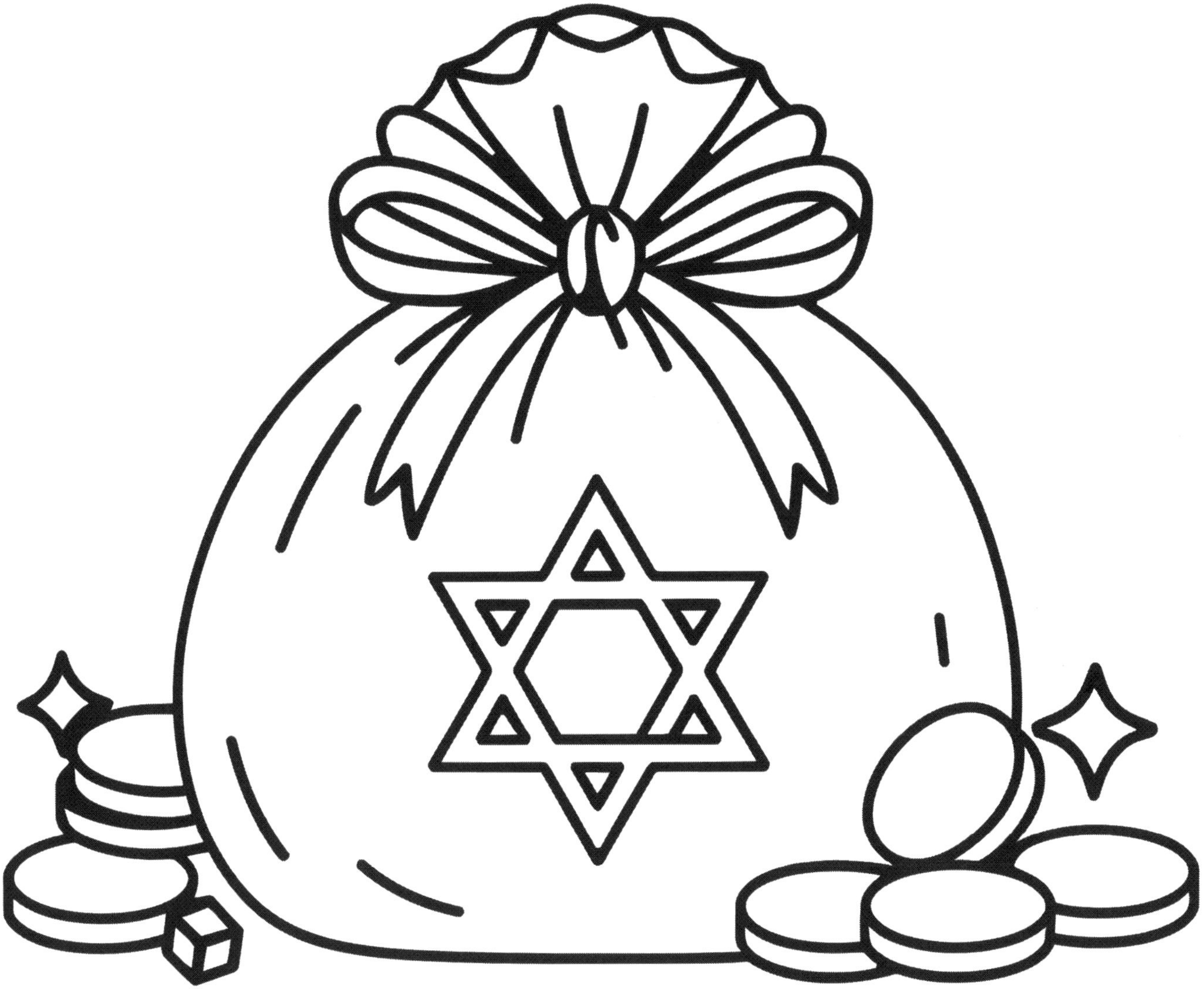

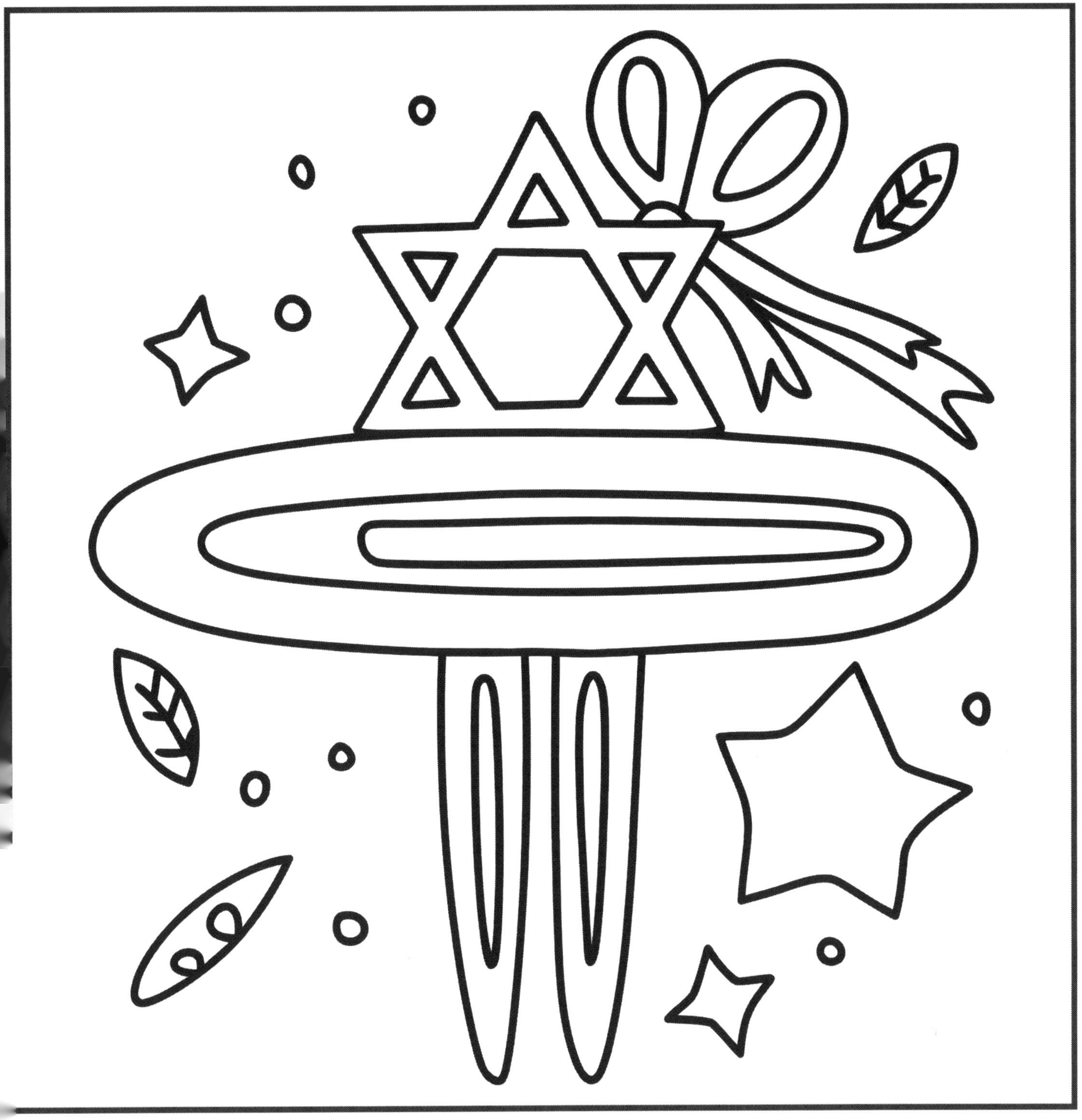

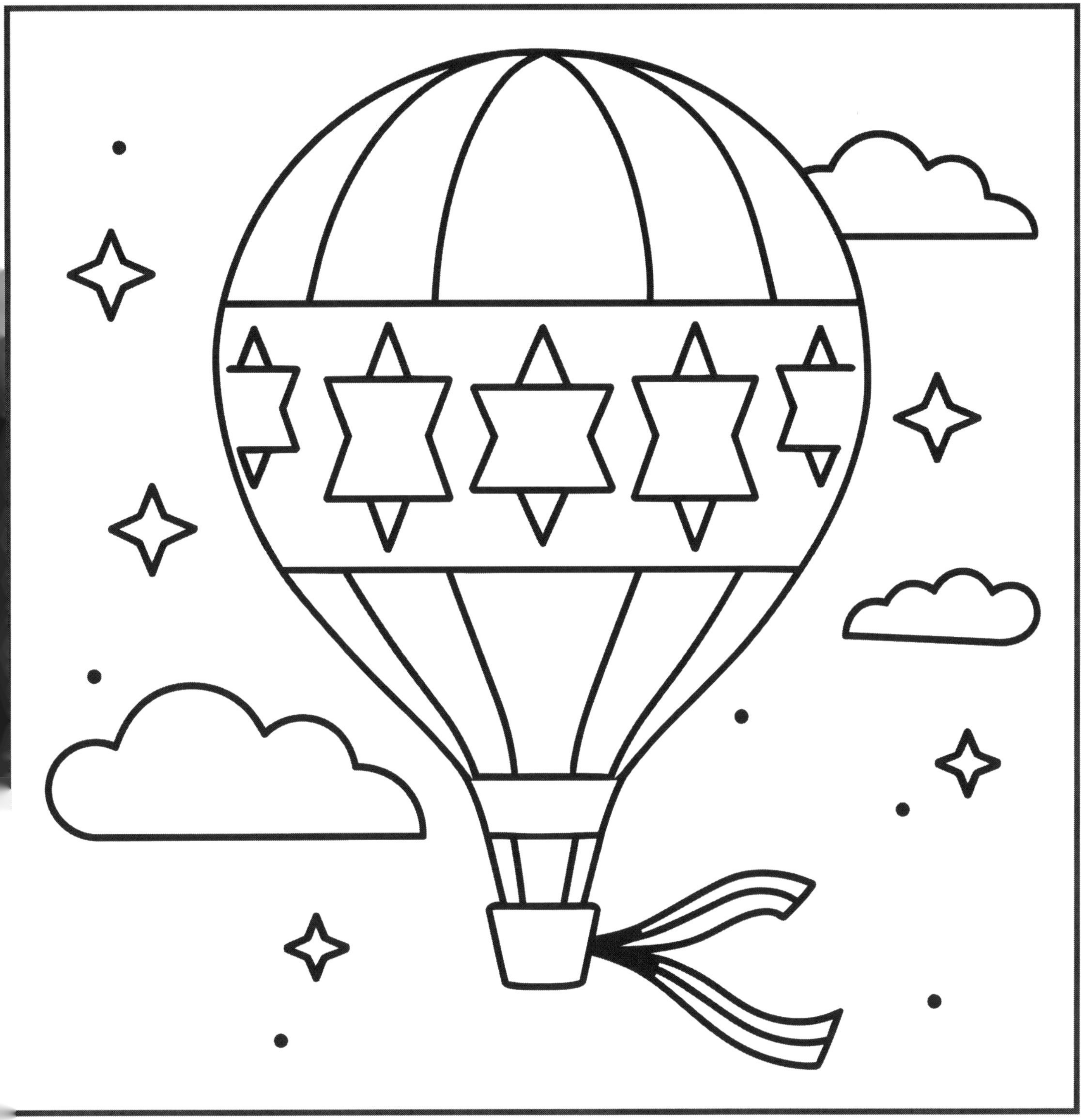

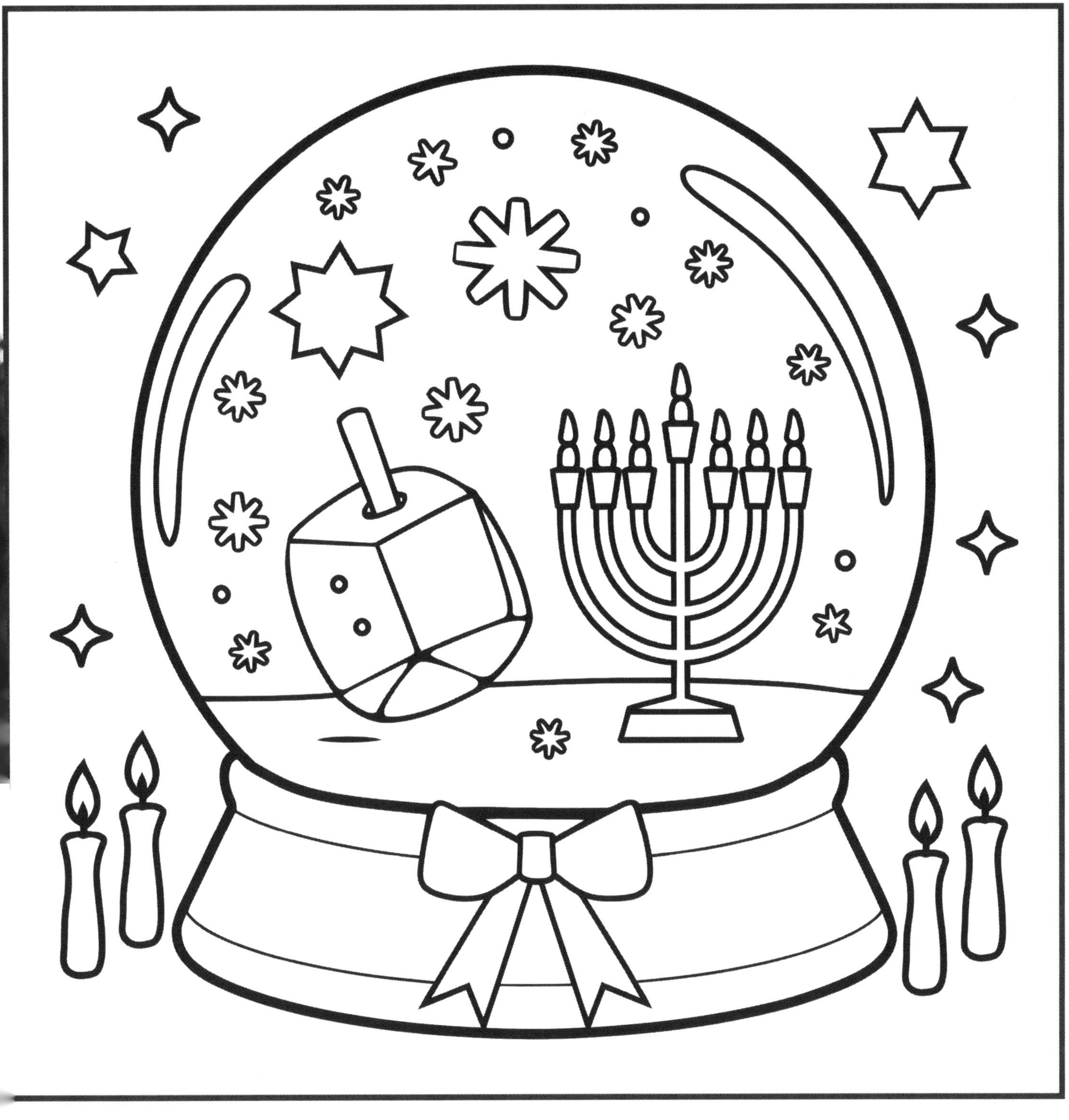

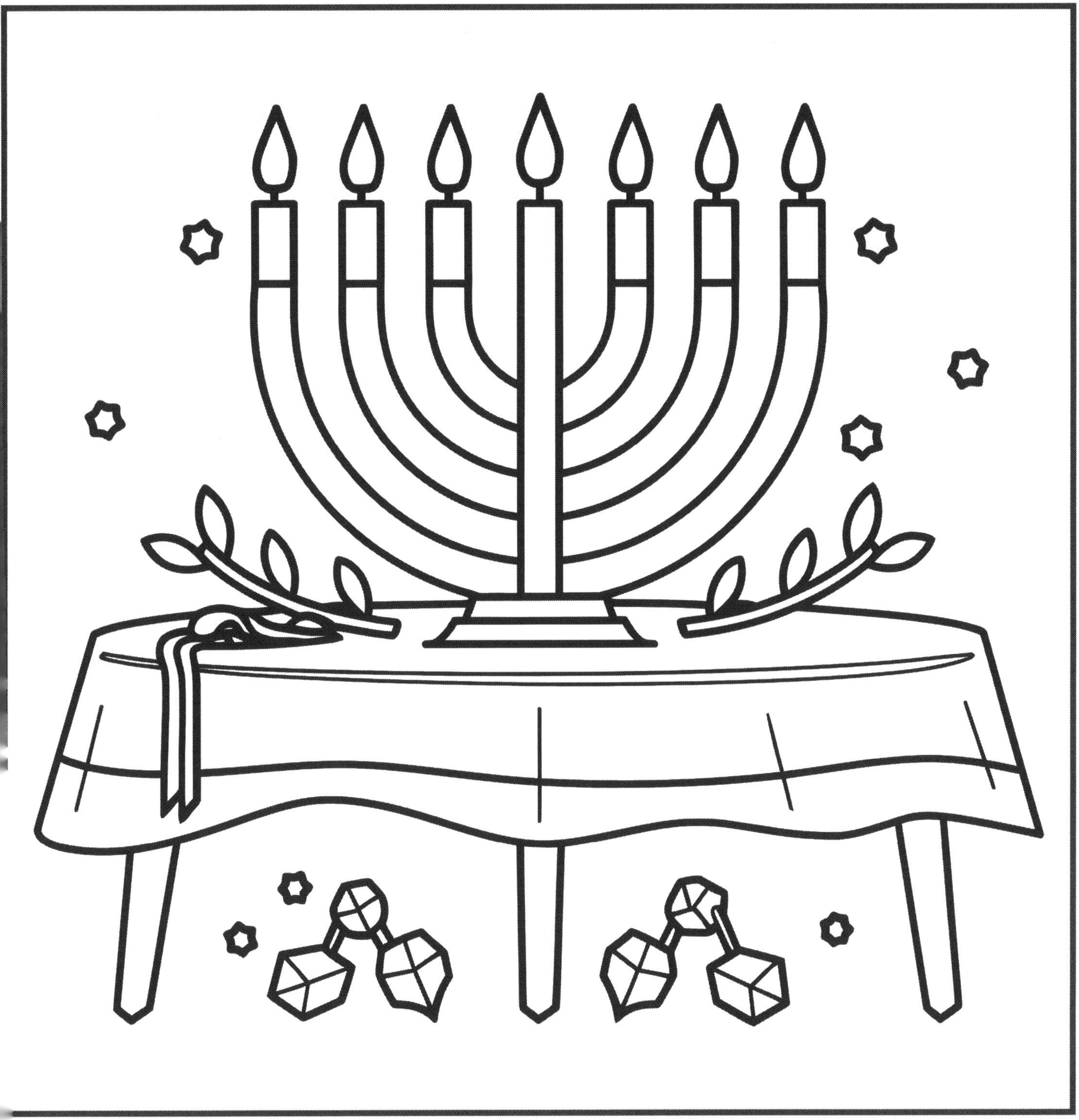

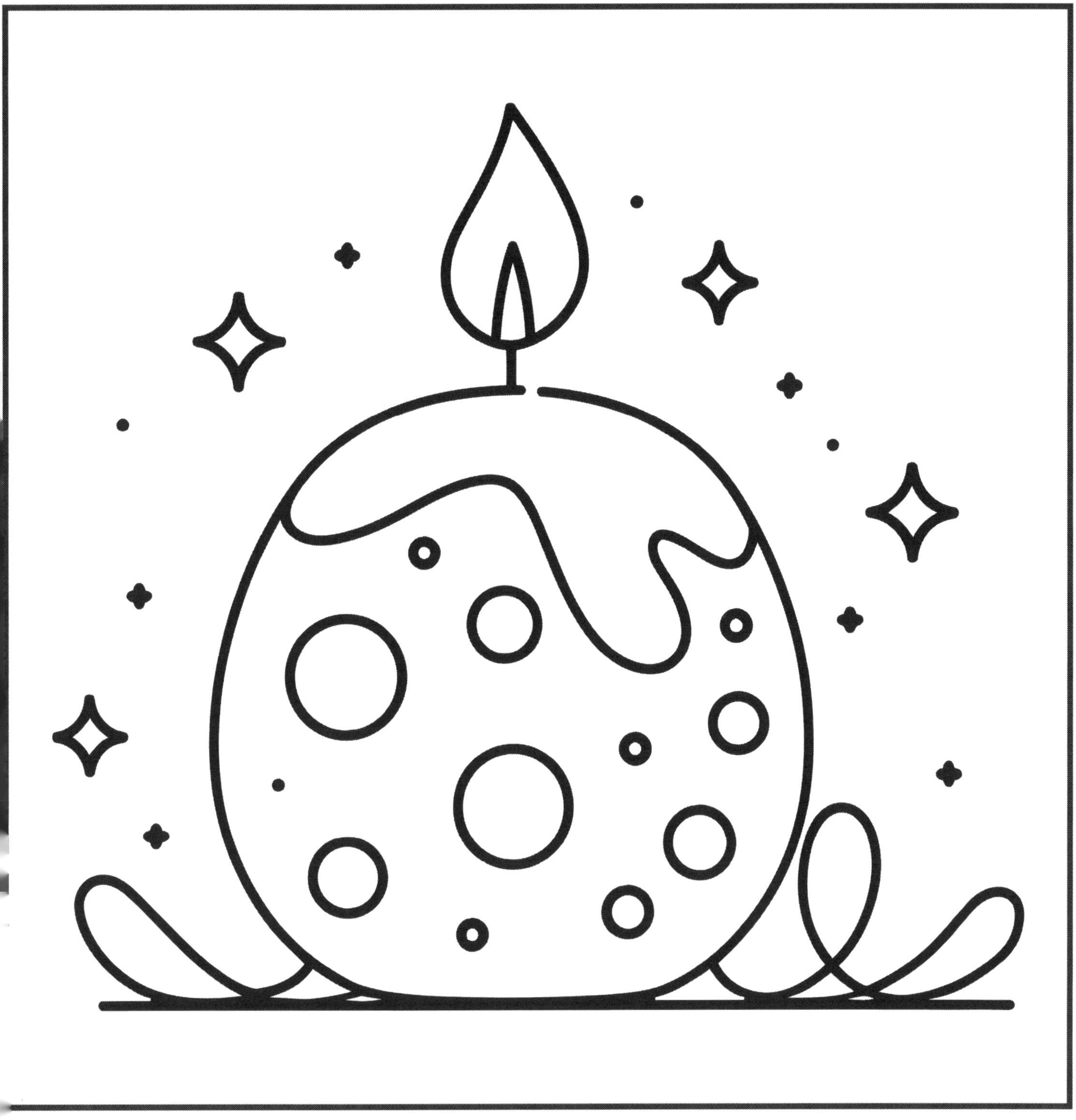

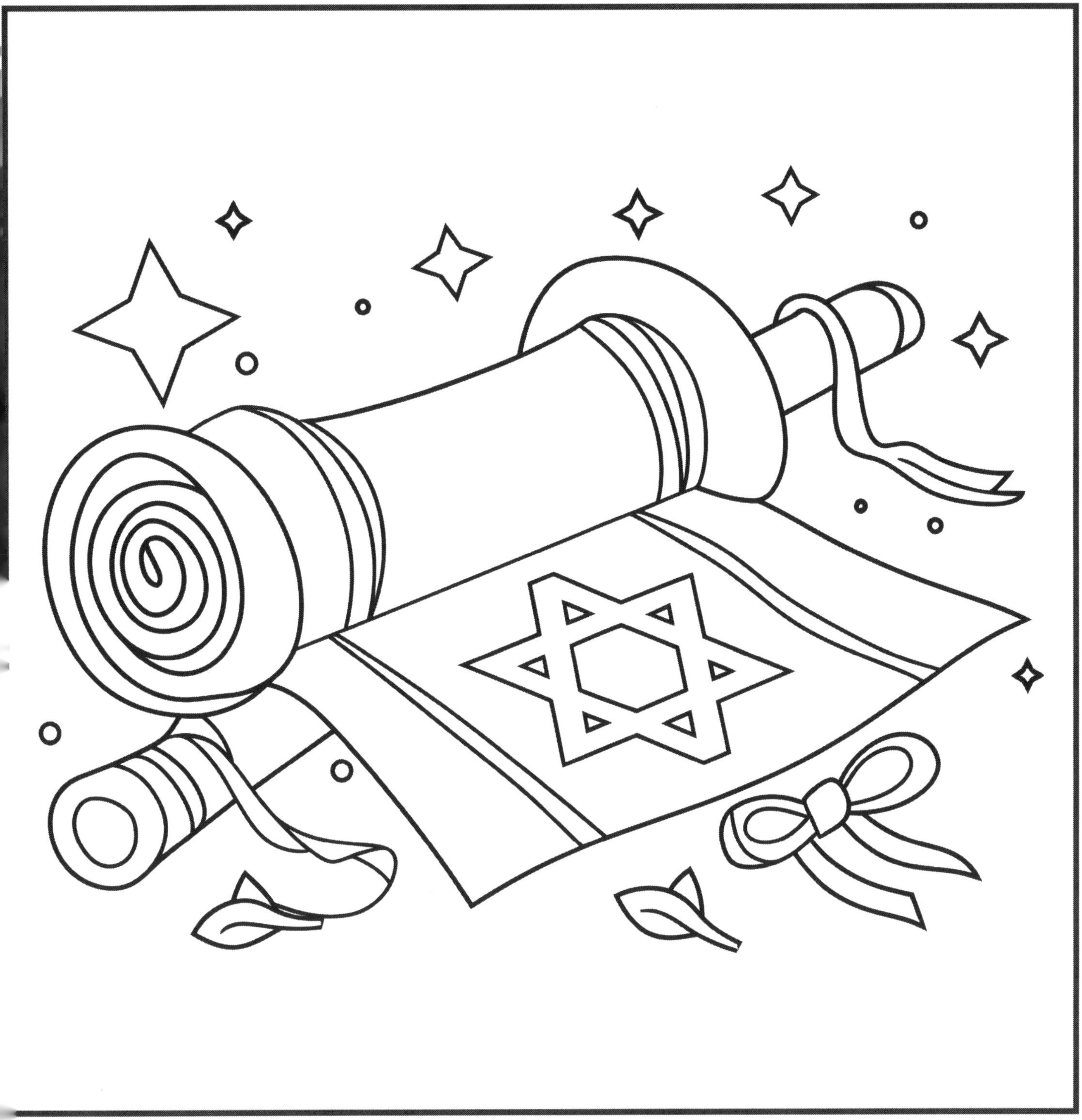

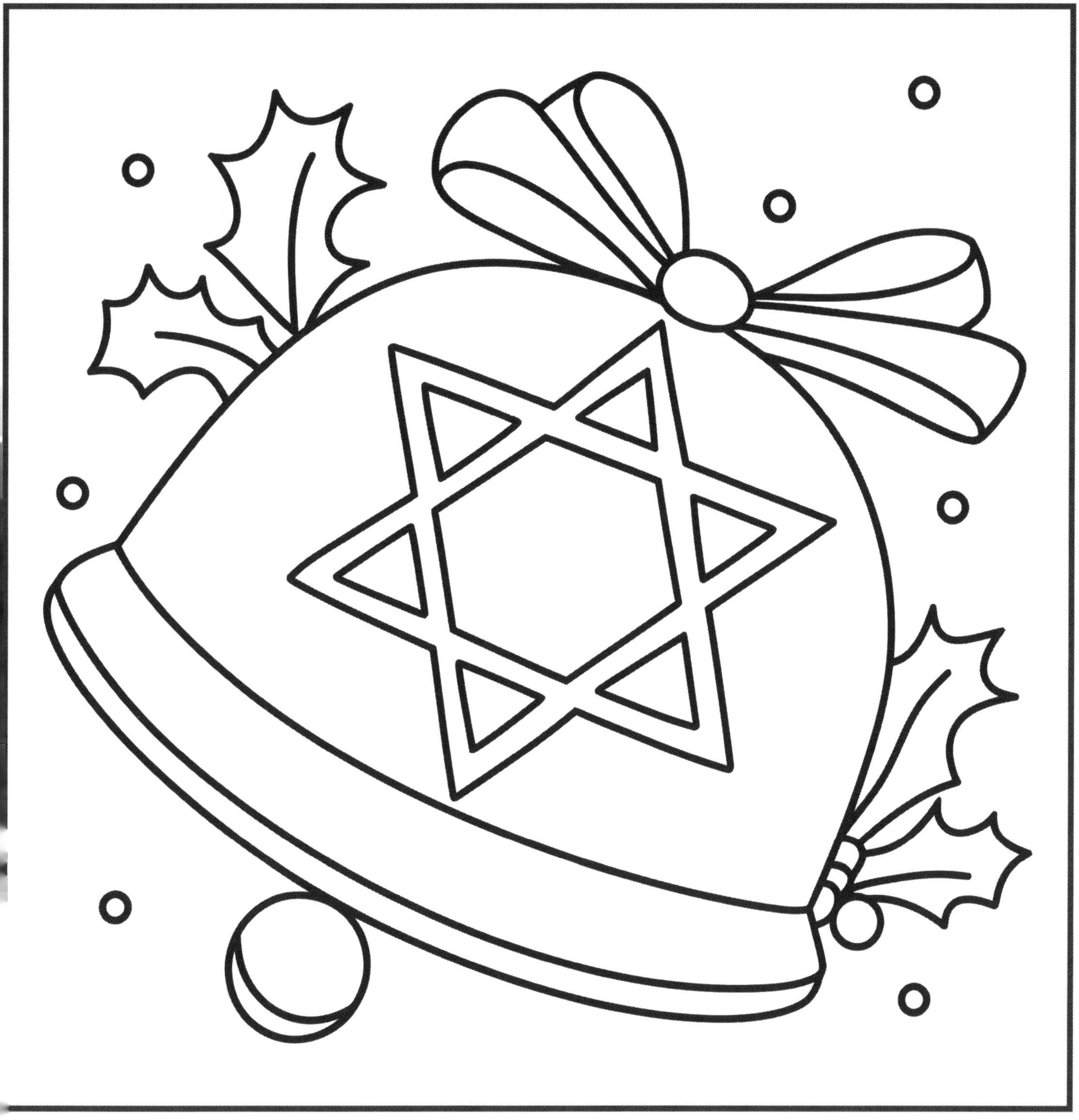

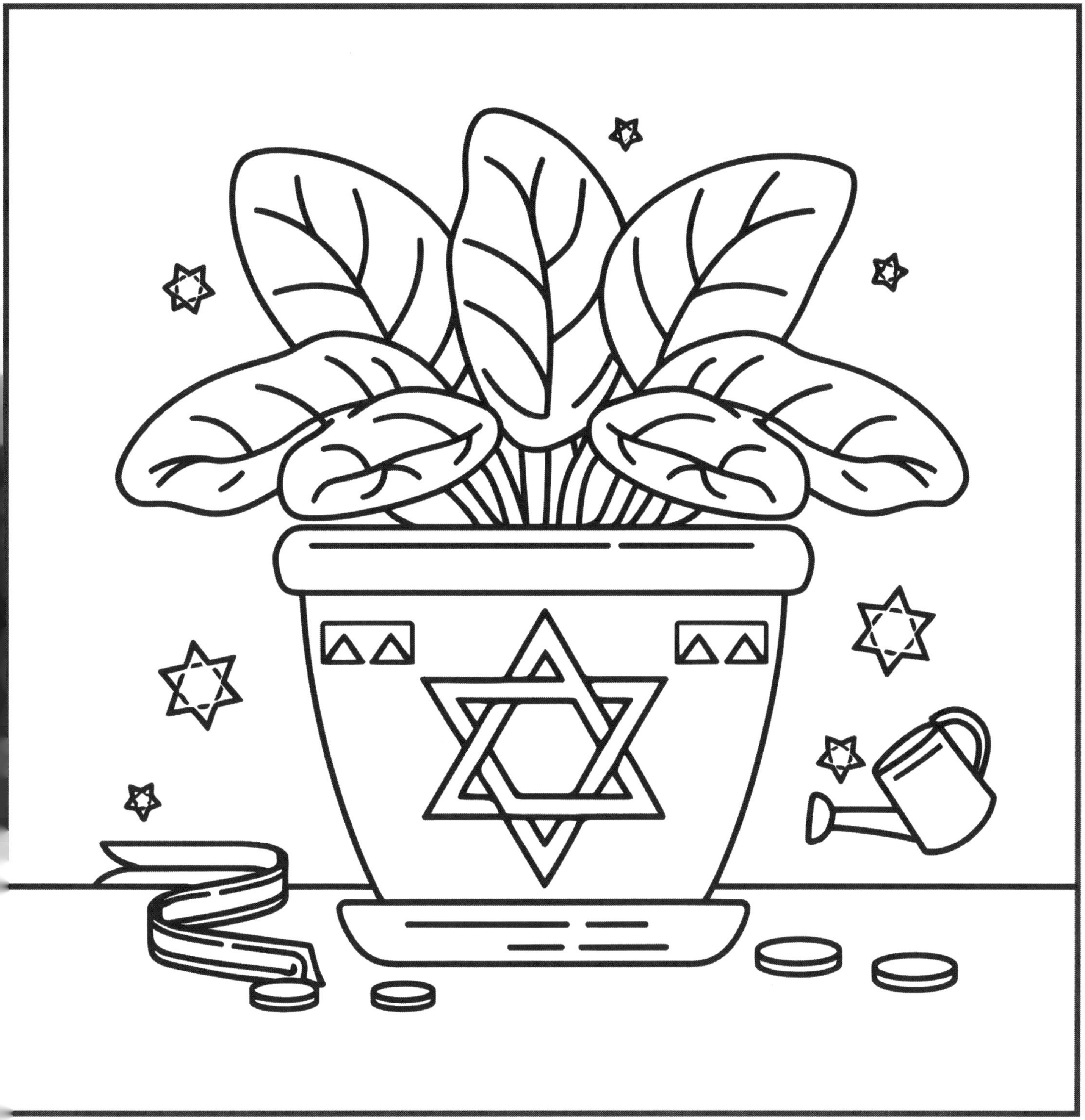

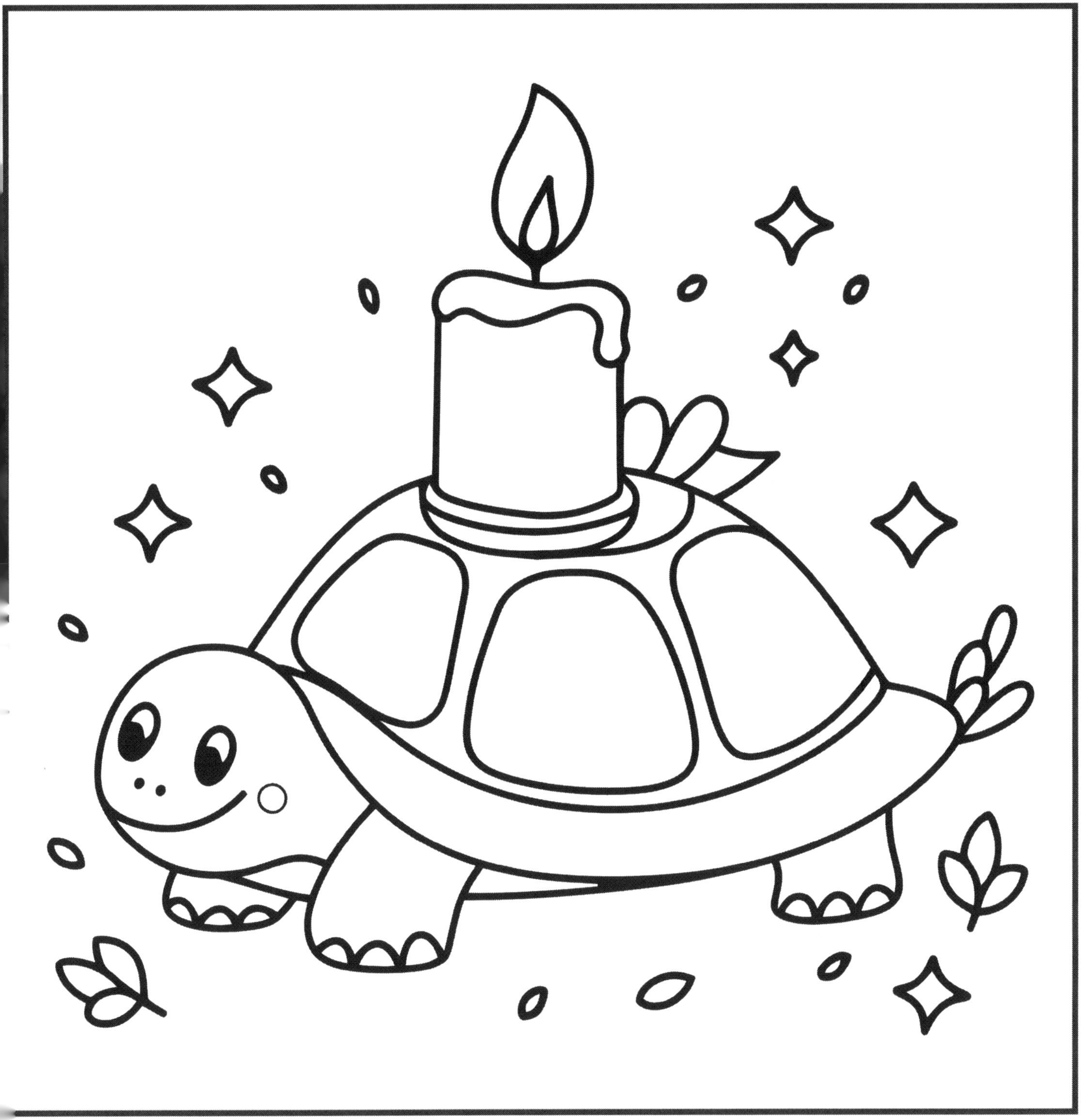

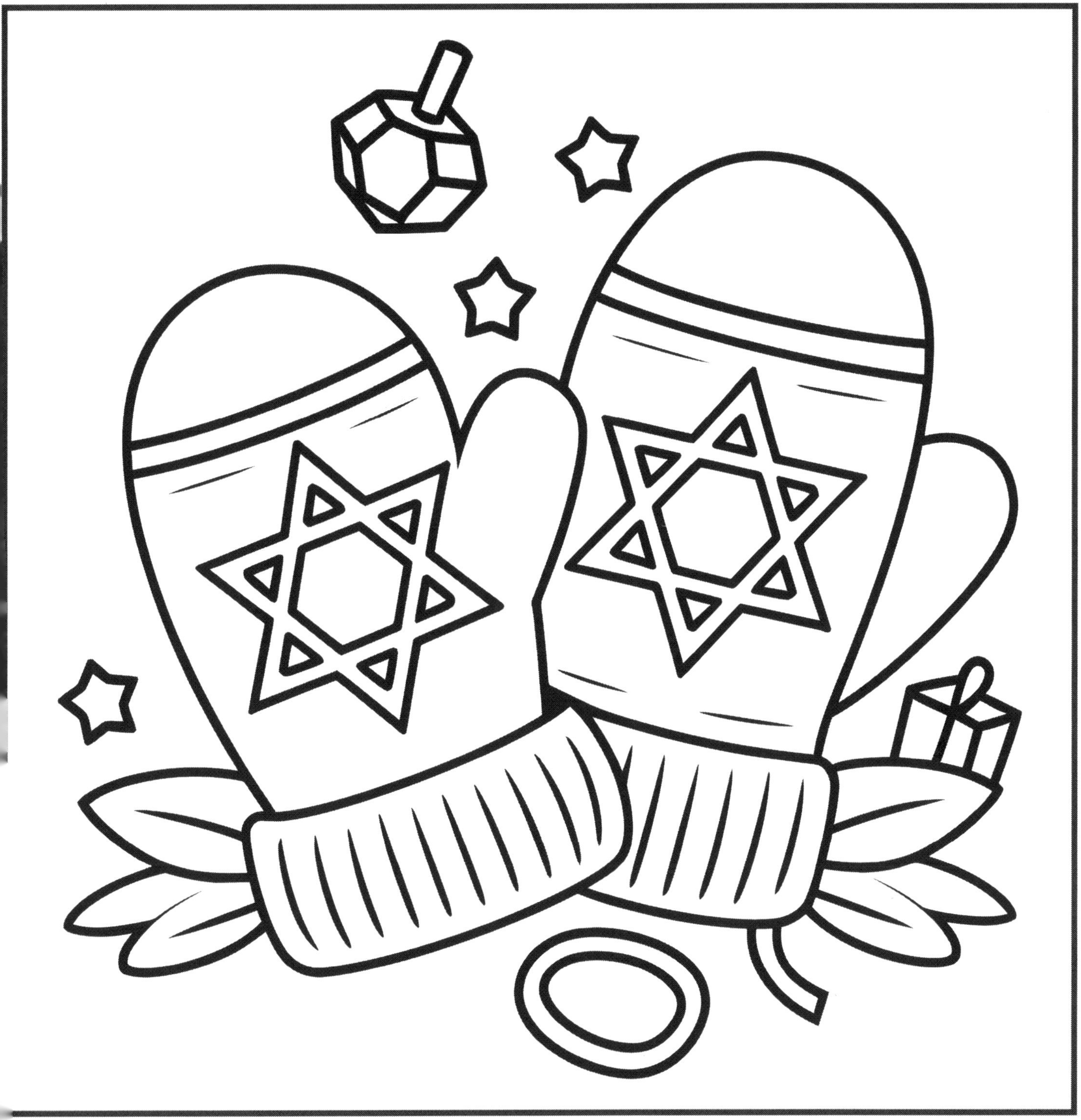

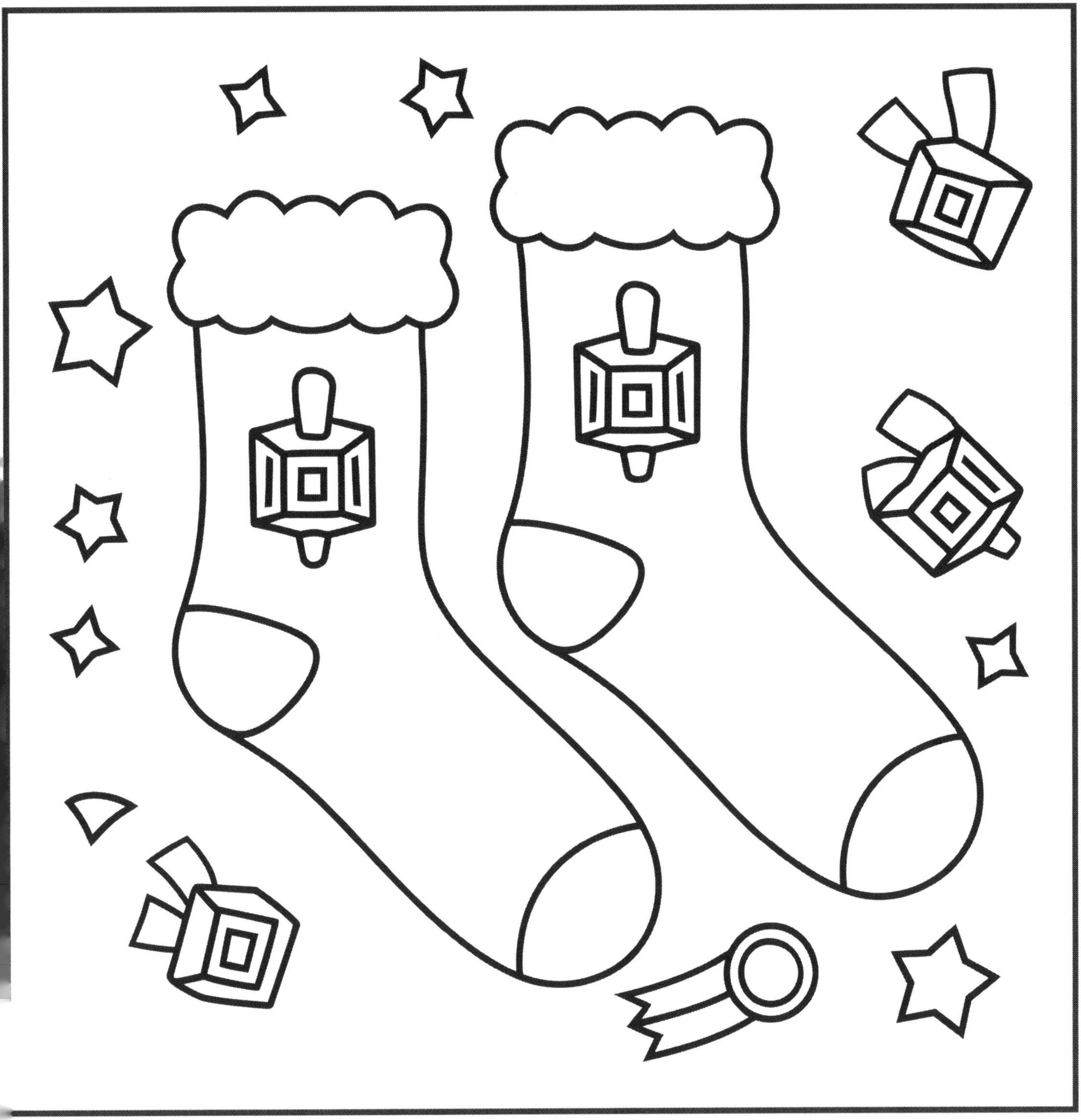

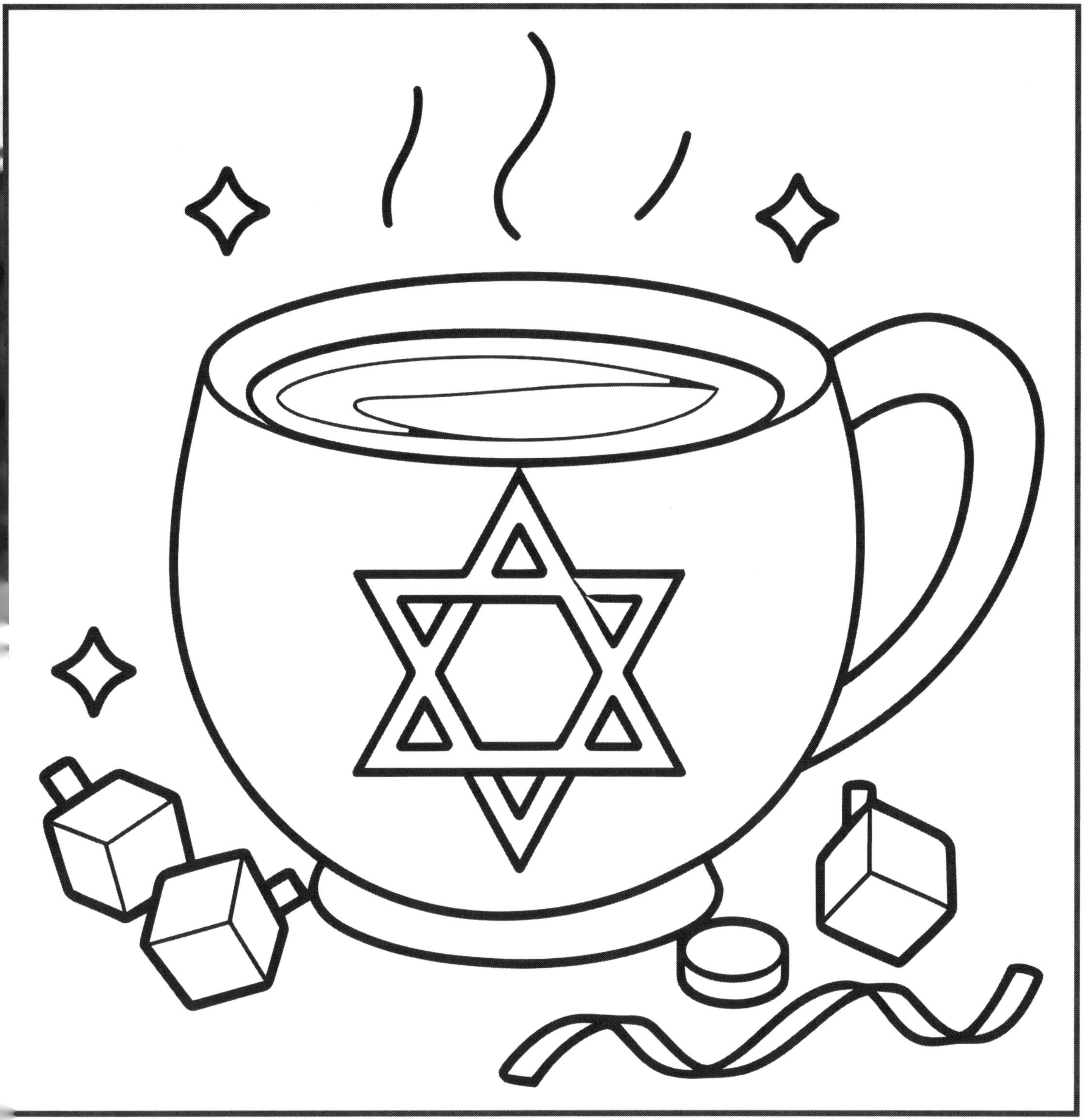

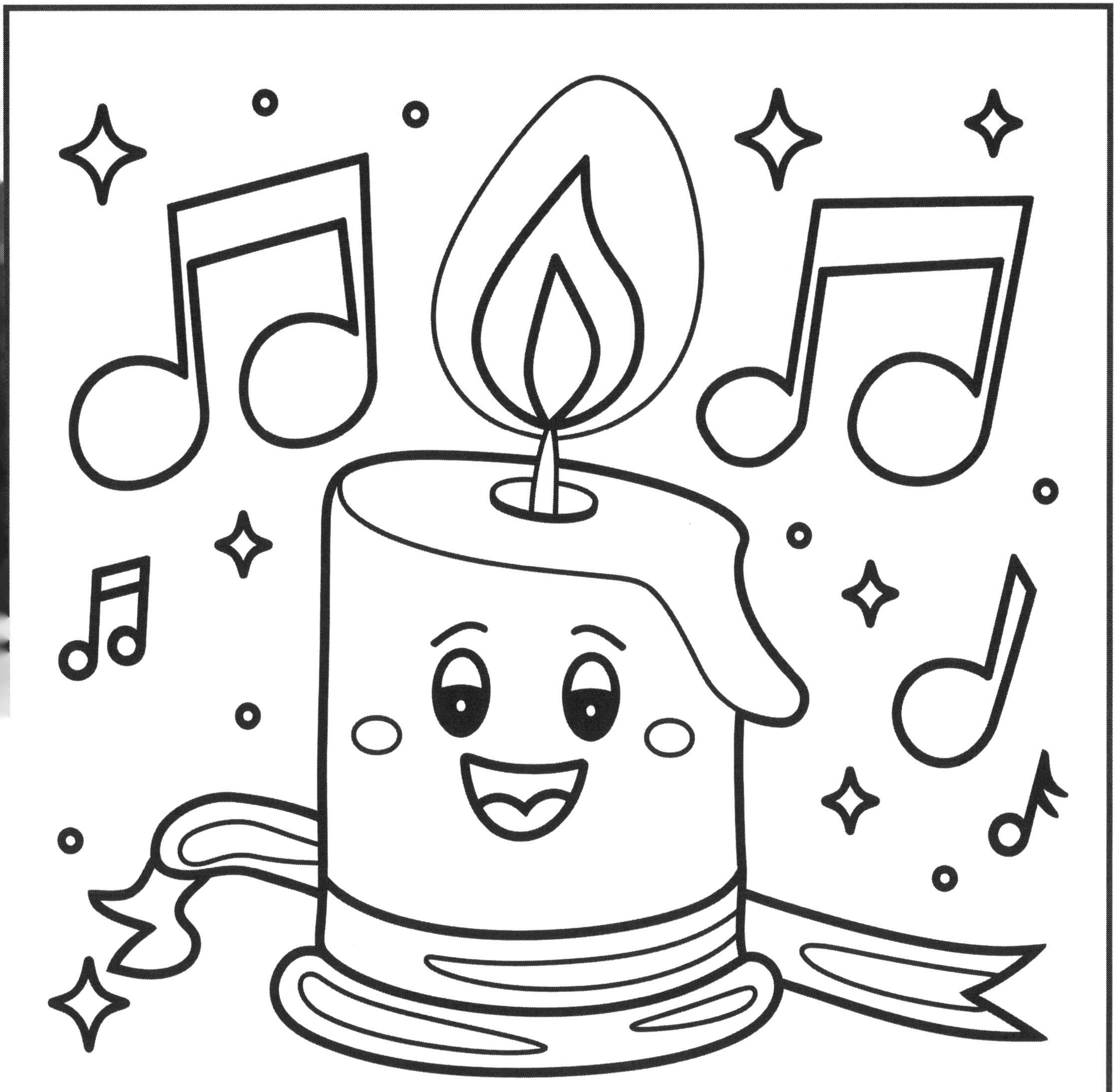

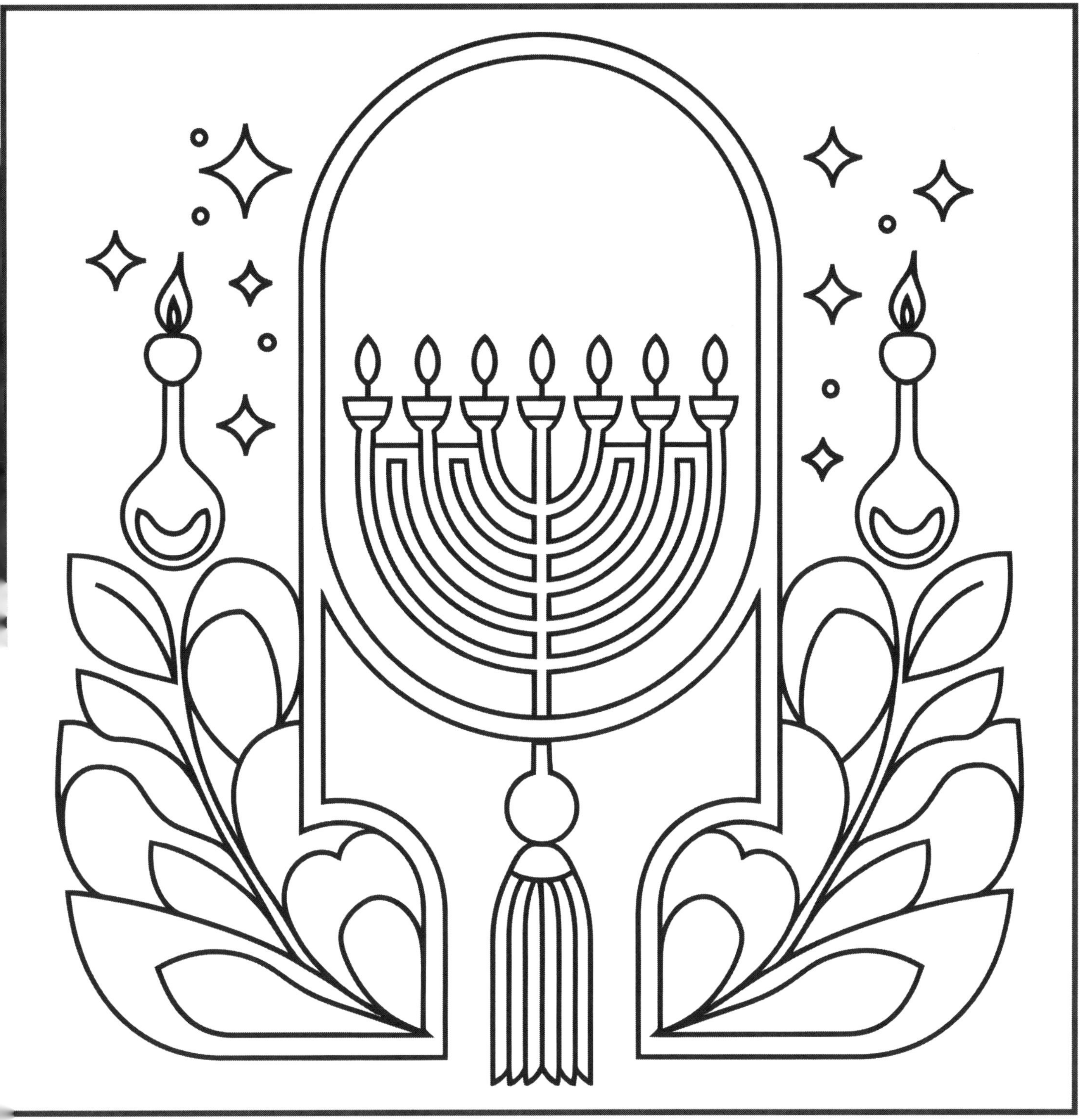

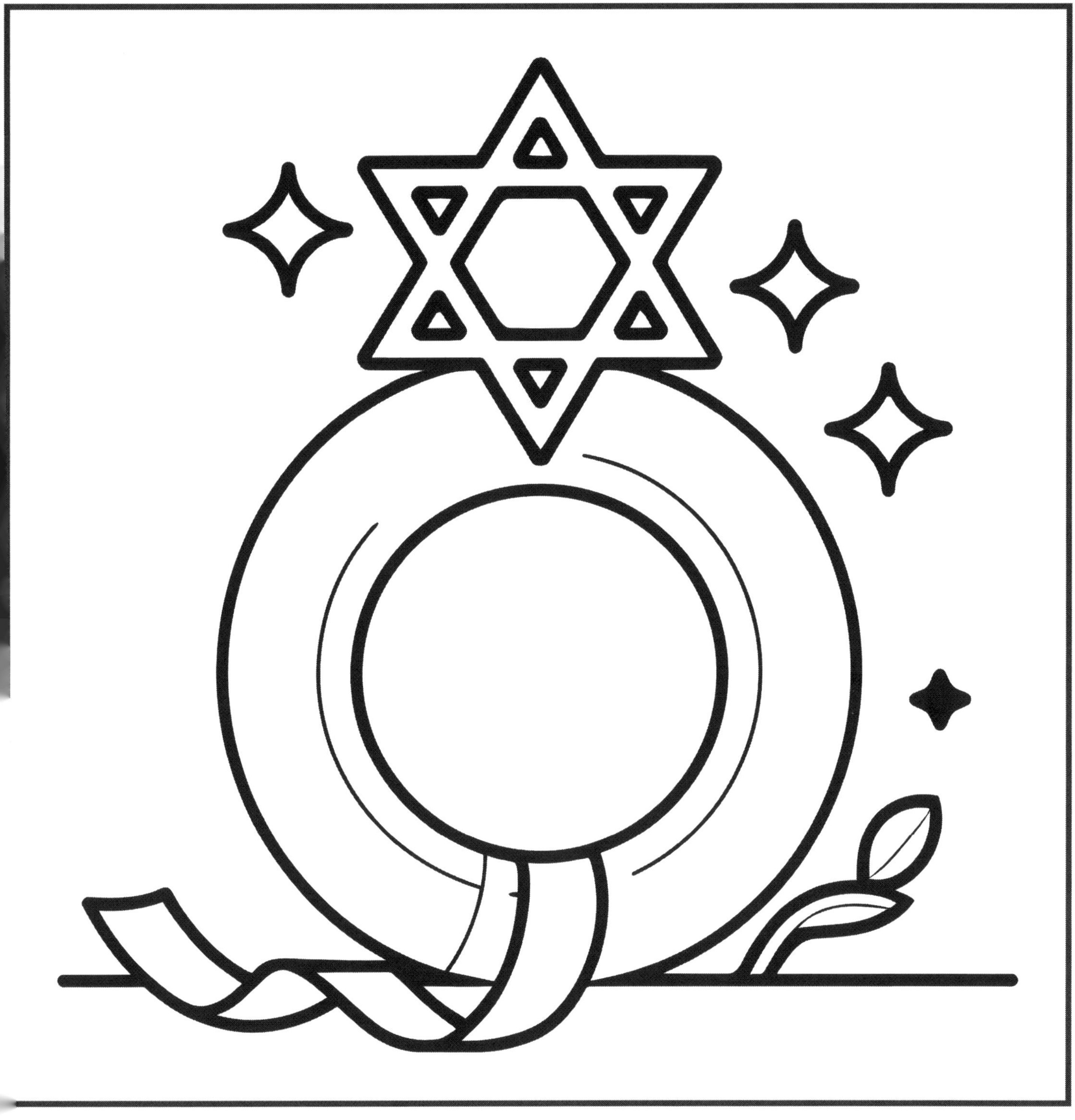

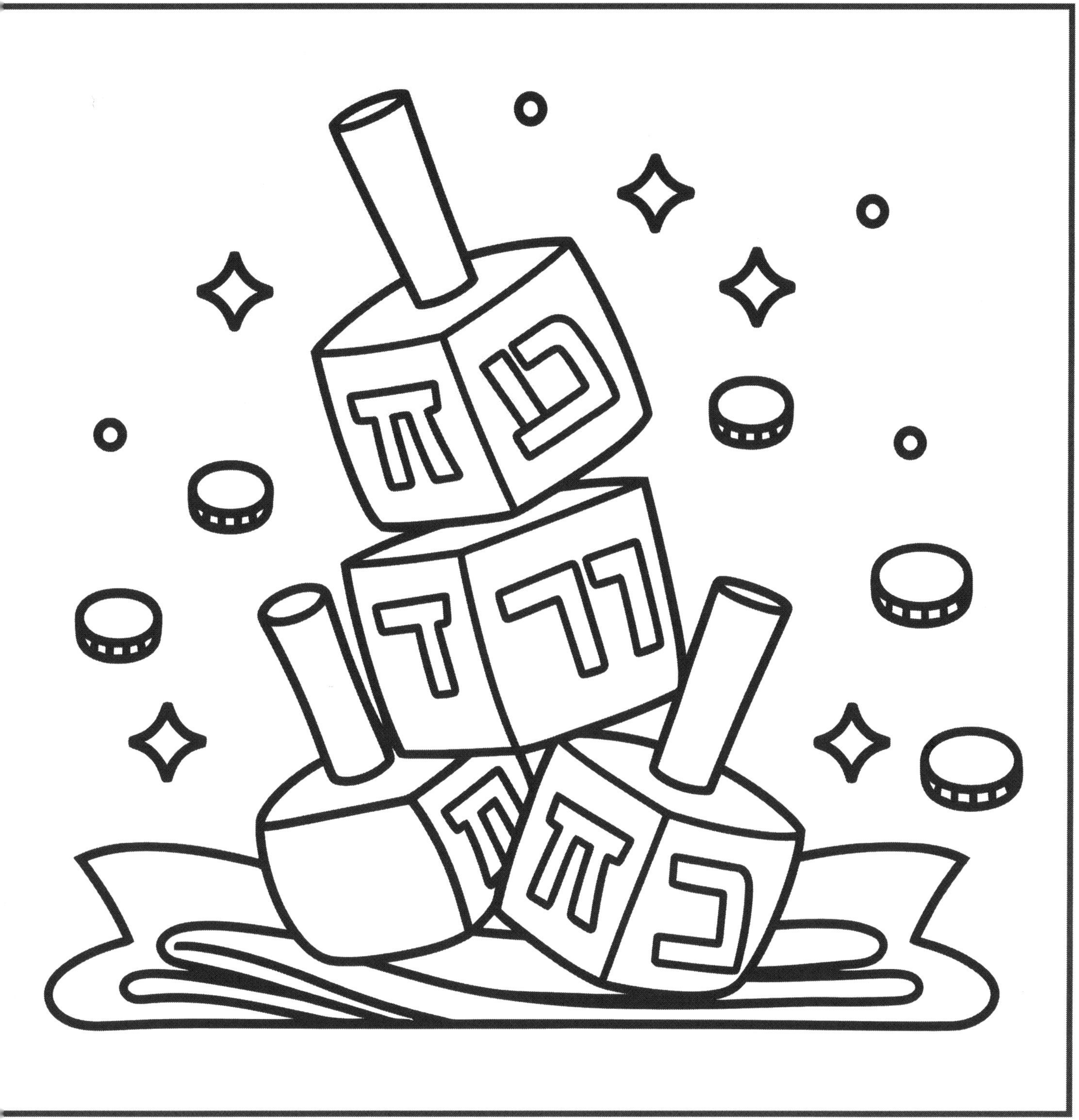

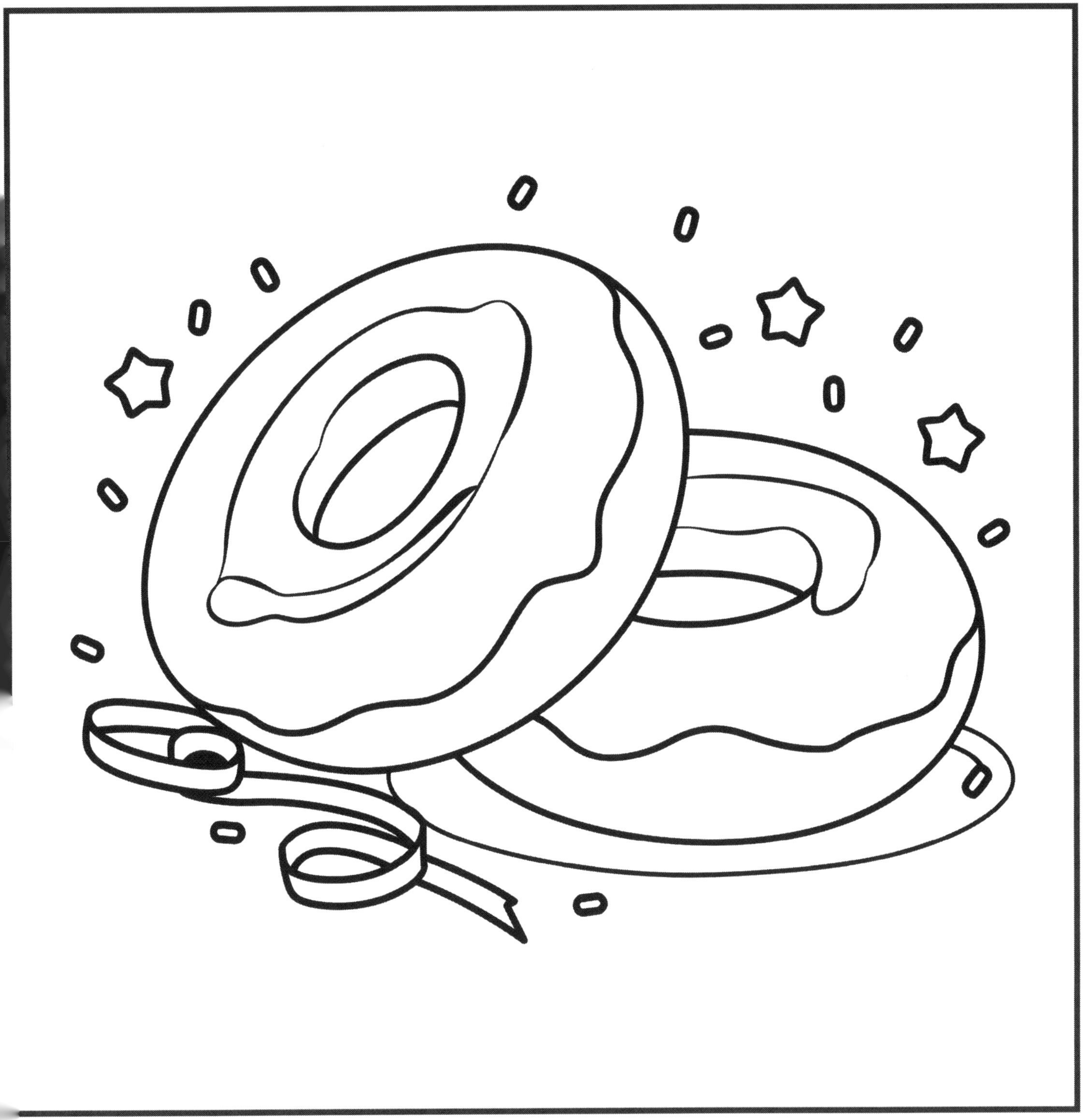

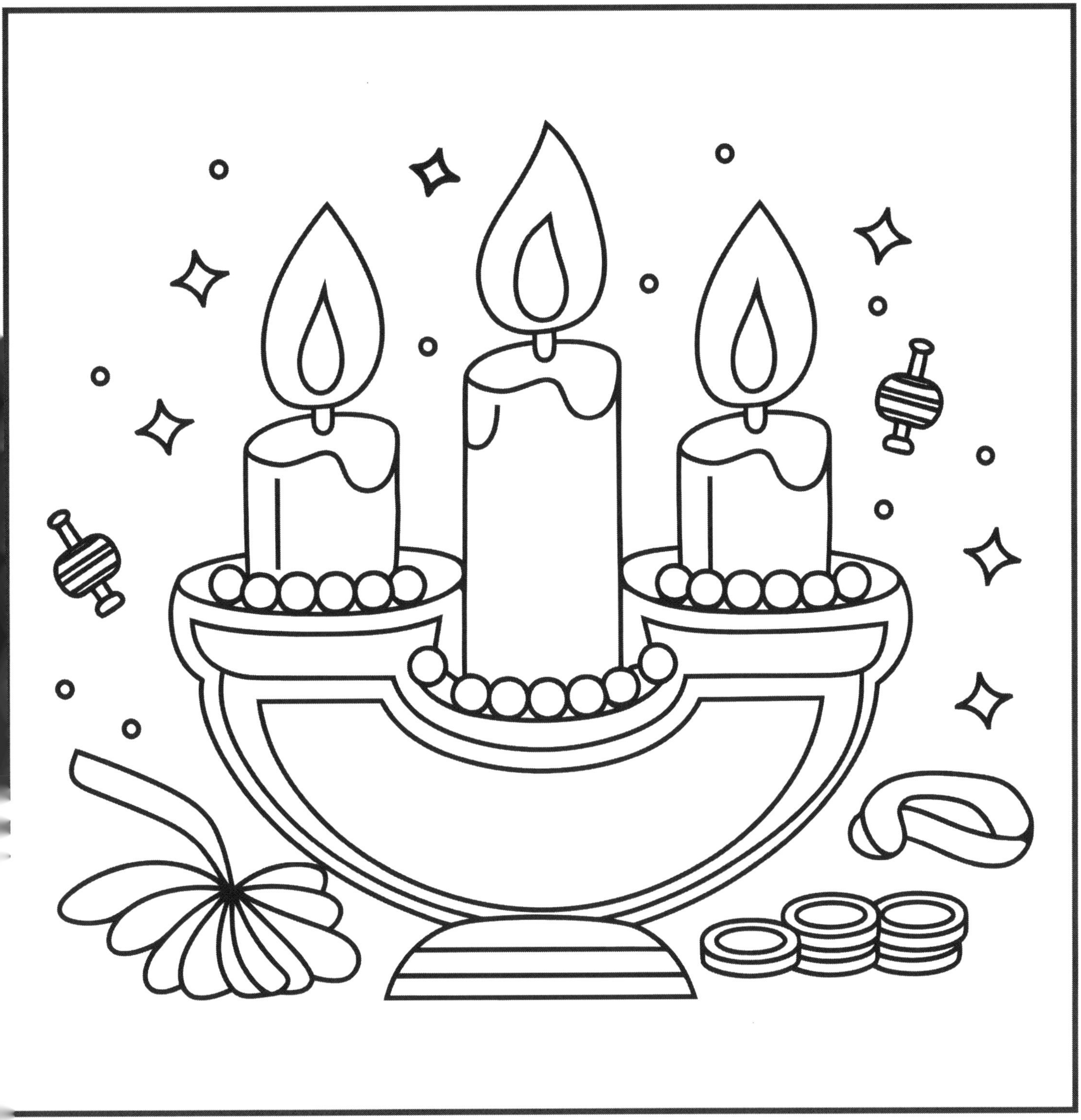

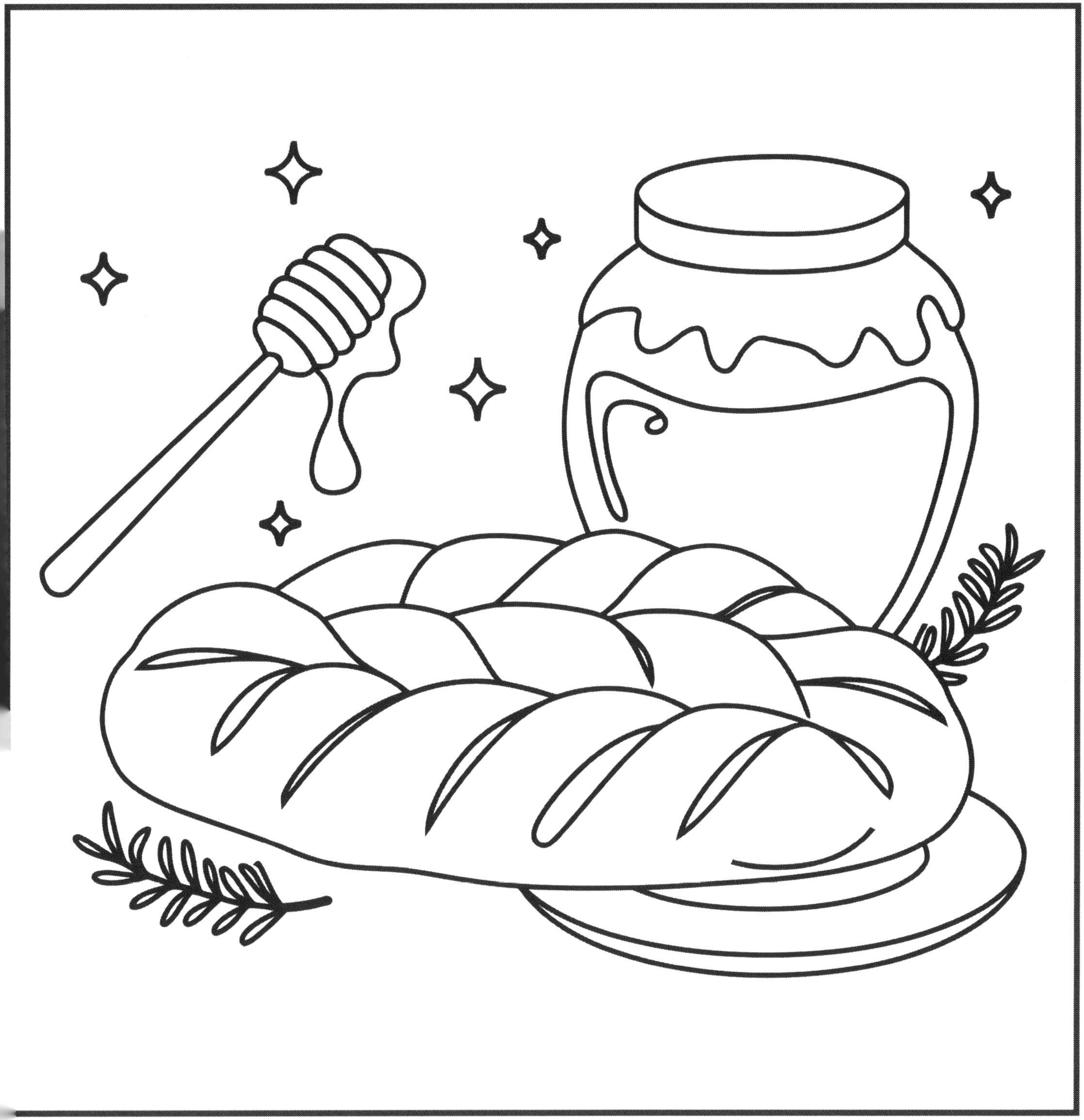

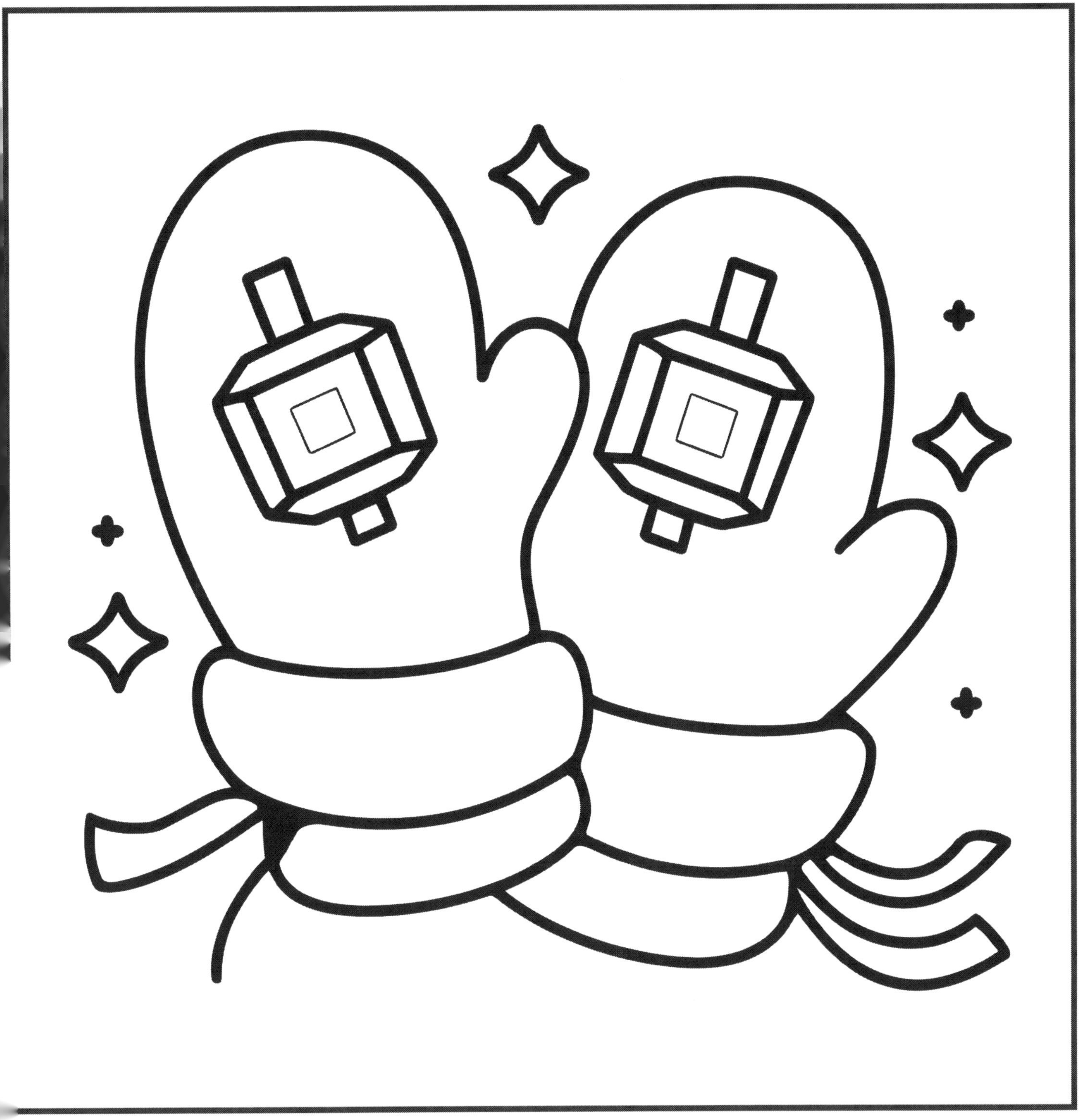

Made in United States
Orlando, FL
21 December 2024

56333546R00057